TABLE OF CONTENTS

ACRONYMS

AMSA	Arctic Marine Shipping Assessment
CIRES	Cooperative Institute for Research in Environmental Sciences
CRS	Congressional Research Service
DEW	Distant Early Warning
EEZ	Exclusive Economic Zone
EIA	Energy Information Agency
EU	European Union
ICBM	Intercontinental Ballistic Missile
IPCC	International Panel on Climate Change
NASA	National Aeronautics and Space Administration
NATO	North Atlantic Treaty Organization
NEP	Northeast Passage
NOAA	National Oceanic and Atmospheric Administration
NORAD	North American Air Defense
NSIDC	National Snow and Ice Data Center
NSF	National Science Foundation
NSPD-66	National Security Presidential Directive 66
NSR	Northern Sea Route
NWP	Northwest Passage
PRC	Peoples Republic of China
SAMS	School of Advanced Military Studies
SLOC	Sea Lines of Communication
SSI	Strategic Studies Institute
UN	United Nations
UNCLOS	United Nations Convention on the Law of the Sea
USARAK	United States Army Alaska
USGS	United States Geological Survey

FIGURES

TABLES

INTRODUCTION

Only when the ice breaks will you truly know who is your friend and who is your enemy.[1]

Inuit proverb

The littoral nations of the Arctic region face potential challenges and opportunities due to climate change. What impact will these changes have on security in the region in the near future? Is there an increase in commercial and military activity in the region, leading to potential increased tension? The polar ice caps that normally cover the North Pole and Arctic Sea through most of the year are receding due to climate change.[2] The question is not if the climate is changing in the Arctic, or its cause, but what are the impacts of receding Arctic ice to international tension or crisis? The reduction of the ice is revealing the potential opportunities and riches in natural resources that now draw the attention of global powers, and raising security concerns in the region.

This growing international interest may generate some alarmist writing among experts using clichéd titles such as, "Arctic Cold War,"[3] "Arctic Heating Up,"[4] or "New Great Game."[5] Arctic security is a growing concern among neighboring Arctic and non-Arctic nations. The region's increasing accessibility to commercial and military activity, makes it a potential new frontier for wealth, power, and dominance among the most powerful and emergent nations on

---

[1]Heather Conley and Jamie Kraut, *US Strategic Interests in the Arctic* (Washington: CSIS, 2010), 1.

[2]Lisa Alexander et. al., *Working Group I Contribution to the IPCC Fifth Assessment Report Climate Change 2013: The Physical Science Basis*, Summary for Policymakers (Geneva: Intergovernmental Panel on Climate Change, 2013), SPM-5-SPM-6.

[3]Paul Arthur Berkman, "Preventing an Arctic Cold War," *New York Times*, March 12, 2013.

[4]Sonny T. Hatton, Canadian Army, "Canadian Unilateralism in the Arctic: Using Scenario Planning to Help Canada Achieve its Strategic Goals in the North" (Monograph, School of Advanced Military Studies, 2013), 1.

[5]Robert Sibley, "Arrival of China in Arctic puts Canada on Alert," *Ottawa Citizen*, October 28, 2011.

1

earth. Nations that border the Arctic, nations near the Arctic, and non-Arctic nations are increasing their activity seeking new deposits of oil, natural gas and minerals that may become economically viable with the receding ice. New ice-free shipping routes are also emerging. The famed Northwest Passage (NWP) once eluded European explorers seeking an alternate sea route from the Atlantic to Pacific Oceans. Some climate change models anticipate the NWP's opening to shipping by 2050.[6] Polar ice measurements in 2007 determined that the route through Canada's northern archipelago is partially ice-free through the summer months and accessible to specialized icebreaker ships.[7] Russia's own Northern Sea Route (NSR) along its northern coast is another potential ice-free sea line of communication (SLOC). Both lanes could shorten shipping length, time, and costs between globalized markets of Europe, Asia and North America.[8] Such new opportunities out of the Arctic region's changing geography are drawing the interests of a globalizing world. This growing world interest, and the lack of political and legal regulation, may lead to an increase in tension, or possibility of crisis or conflict.[9] Old, often ignored, territorial disputes between the Arctic littoral nations are becoming contentious with the possibility of resource wealth or shipping opportunities.[10] Some of the world's more powerful and wealthy nations, Russia, Canada, China, and the United States race to measure the potential opportunities worth seizing and increase their militarization to secure their stake of the Arctic region.

---

[6]Laurence C. Smith and Scott R. Stephenson, "New Trans-Arctic shipping routes navigable by midcentury," *Proceedings of the National Academy of Science of the United States of America*, vol. 110 no. (2013): E1191-E1195.

[7]National Snow and Ice Data Center, "Arctic Sea Ice News, Fall 2007," www.nsidc.org (accessed May 15, 2014).

[8]Ibid., E1191-E1195.

[9]Berkman, "Preventing an Arctic Cold War."

[10]Ibid.

2

Organization of Paper

This study has five sections. The introduction notes the increased interest in the Arctic region. Section two is the literature review regarding the environment, defining the Arctic region, relevant state and non-state actors, their interests and desires in the Arctic region, and considerations for scenario planning. Section 3 is the methodology related to the parameters and theories regarding the creation of scenarios forecasting potential futures of Arctic security. Section 4 is the proposed scenarios forecasting the near future of the Arctic region based on the analysis. Section 5 summarizes the study, and provides recommendations for shaping the Arctic region's future from potential crisis to stability. The recommendations frame along operational approaches toward mitigating conflict and promoting cooperation.

LITERATURE REVIEW

The receding polar ice in the Arctic resulting from climate change is altering the region's geography. Increased commercial shipping through possible opening of waterways, and newly accessible natural resources are generating great interest with expanded exploration and presence by state and non-state actors.[11] Geographic and economic trends may lead to security issues among the littoral neighbors and outer nations of the Arctic region. Among these nations are lingering territorial disputes rising in importance as new hydrocarbon resources and SLOCs are discovered. These countries, and their governments, face decisions on strategies serving their interests in the region. Interested nations can decide on approaches in the Arctic of cooperation or competition to secure their interests. National actors can participate through multi-national forums and agreements to distribute the region's riches for mutual benefit. Able statecraft and diplomacy can allow the open and peaceful use of disputed waterways and territory for

---

[11]Ibid.

3

international commerce.[12] Certain powerful nations with advantages of economic and military might and fortunes of geography are better able to pursue unilateral or hegemonic approaches in the Arctic region. Forces of nationalist pride and sovereignty can lead to a race to seize and secure the Arctic access and wealth for their own prosperity.[13] Arctic stakeholders are deciding on the future of the Arctic in response to changing climate. Will it be a trend toward a tranquil future, or rising tension or crisis as nations seek greater shares of the potential wealth?

Research Question

What is the potential for crisis or conflict in the Arctic Sea region? This study will examine the possibilities for increased tensions leading to crises or conflicts in the Arctic region over the near term. Whether a potential crisis or conflict is more or less likely, this study will look at operational approaches to fulfill strategic goals to mitigate crises in the Arctic region. This study will examine the factors, trends, indicators, and variables that may contribute to the outcome variable of potential increase in crisis or conflict conditions in the Arctic region. The defined outcome variable is the level of anticipated tension or crisis in the Arctic region. This study examines prominent variables and trends regarding the changes in the Arctic region's geography from climate change. The study further scrutinizes the increased interests of wealthy, powerful state and non-state actors in the Arctic to determine if there is an increased likelihood of future tension or conflict. This data helps build scenarios to allow better forecasts for the near future security of the Arctic region.

---

[12]Michael Byers, *Who Owns the Arctic?: Understanding Sovereignty Disputes in the North* (Vancouver: Douglas and McIntyre, 2009), Kindle Electronic Edition, Location 1891-1909.

[13]Scott G. Borgerson, "Arctic Meltdown," *Foreign Affairs*, (March/April 2008).

Defining the Arctic Region

Geography

The study of security issues in the Arctic requires clarity in the definitions of the region, and its geographical parameters. The Arctic region is the maritime region consisting of the Arctic Ocean surrounded by the northern coasts of Europe, Asia, and North America. The ocean area is slightly less than 1.5 times the size of the continental United States, and covered by a perennial drifting polar icepack that, on average, is about 3 meters thick.[14] Any area where water stays in solid form as snow or ice is known as the cryosphere. There are three scientific definitions of the Arctic region's boundaries.[15] The most noted boundary of the Arctic is the region above the Arctic Circle, the imaginary line that circles the globe at 66° 32" N, depicted by the blue dashed line in figure 1. The Arctic Circle marks the latitude above which the sun does not set below the horizon during the summer solstice, and does not rise on the winter equinox.[16] Another scientific definition of the Arctic is the Arctic tree line where the environment transitions to the Arctic tundra biome depicted by the green line in figure 1. The Arctic tundra region is composed of perennial frozen soil, called permafrost. The permafrost hinders tree growth and only allows small shrubs and lichen vegetation.[17] The third definition of the Arctic is temperature, or the 10-degree isotherm line, depicted by the red line in figure 1. This area is the high latitude region where the average daily summer temperature does not rise above 10 degrees Celsius, or 50 degrees Fahrenheit.[18] This more expansive definition of the Arctic region encompasses most of

---

[14]Central Intelligence Agency, "World Factbook: Arctic Ocean," www.cia.gov (accessed November 8, 2013).

[15]National Snow and Ice Data Center, "All About Arctic Climatology and Meteorology," www.nsidc.org (accessed November 8, 2013).

[16]Ibid.

[17]Ibid.

[18]Ibid.

the region defined by the other two scientific definitions.[19] This study will use the 10-degree isotherm line to define the Arctic region. Using the 10-degree isotherm line matters as its boundaries extend to maritime straits such as the Bering and Davis Straits. Both straits are vital accesses to the Arctic region and its sea passages. Control of these maritime accesses within the 10-degree isotherm line may prove as crucial to the Arctic as the Malacca Strait and Suez Canal are vital to global security and commerce.[20]

The extreme polar climate of the Arctic keeps the region remote and sparsely populated. There are approximately four million people living in the Arctic region, many are distinct groups found only in the Arctic who have subsisted off the land for thousands of years.[21] The harsh conditions disincentivize encroachment of populations and commercial and military activity. Most activity from outside of the Arctic is limited to scientific research.

---

[19]Ibid.

[20]US Energy Information Administration (EIA), "World Oil Transit Chokepoints, Analysis," www.eia.gov (accessed March 9, 2014).

[21]Arctic Council, "Peoples of the Arctic," www.arctic-council.org (accessed March 9, 2014).

Figure 1: Map of the Arctic region depicting the three definitions of the Arctic: the Arctic Circle, the tree line, and the 10-degree isotherm line.

Source: National Snow and Ice Data Center, "All About Arctic Climatology and Meteorology," www.nsidc.org (accessed September 27, 2013).[22]

---

[22]The 10-degree isotherm line, in red, encompasses the Bering Strait between Alaska and the Russian far east; the Davis Strait between Greenland and Baffin Island; and Iceland. All are important for access to the Arctic region.

Changing Climate

A nearly ice-free Arctic Ocean in September before mid-century is *likely*.[23]

Climate Change 2013: The Physical Science Basis

Concerns regarding the extent of Arctic sea ice focus on the speed of polar ice cap recession, and the ability of governments and international regimes to manage any increased human activity. Scientific study first observed changes in the global climate through over a century recorded data.[24] Further climate studies on the Arctic, until within the past decade, did not include security issues, or future tension. Most previous Arctic climate concerns related to wildlife and indigenous peoples.[25] Managing such issues of conservation in the Arctic was the original purpose of forming an international forum among littoral Arctic nations in 1996, known as the Arctic Council.

The changes in the Arctic region and the recession of the polar ice from climate change is closely monitored and studied. The National Snow and Ice Data Center (NSIDC) is an authoritative research body on Arctic ice. The center is part of the Cooperative Institute for Research in Environmental Sciences (CIRES) at the University of Colorado, Boulder. Grants and contracts from US federal agencies such as the National Aeronautics and Space Administration (NASA), National Science Foundation (NSF), and the National Oceanic and Atmospheric Administration (NOAA) support the center and its research.[26] The NSIDC maintains daily updates on sea ice conditions.[27] Its report on Arctic sea ice in September 2013 generated media interest. The report revealed that the lowest extent of Arctic sea ice for summer 2013 was a slight

---

[23]Lisa Alexander et. al., *Climate Change 2013: The Physical Science Basis*, SPM-17.

[24]Ibid., SPM-2-SPM-3.

[25]Arctic Council, "Environment and People," www.arctic-council.org (accessed March 9, 2014).

[26]National Snow and Ice Data Center, "Our Sponsors," www.nsidc.org (accessed March 9, 2014).

[27]National Snow and Ice Data Center, "Arctic Sea Ice News and Analysis," www.nsidc.org (accessed March 9, 2014).

increase from the 2012 summer lowest extent. The past seven seasons were the seven lowest levels of Arctic sea ice according to satellite data records. September 2013 was the sixth lowest on record for summer sea ice levels.[28] Some doubters of climate change seized on this report of growing Arctic ice. A Fox News report on September 9, 2013 described Arctic sea ice as "a whopping 60 percent increase."[29] A New York Times article on the same subject described a 50 percent increase.[30] The NSIDC report expects the trend of receding ice to continue despite the increase in 2013. The new ice, according to the NSIDC, is "first year ice," which is "thinner and more vulnerable to melt," making the increase temporary.[31]

A more comprehensive report from the International Panel on Climate Change (IPCC) of the United Nations, anticipates Arctic sea ice continuing to recede during the 21st century. The IPCC reports with "medium confidence," that Arctic sea ice extent is likely forecasted as "nearly ice-free in September before mid-century" as per some climate models.[32] There is less agreement on exactly when in the 21st century the Arctic will be ice-free in September. The rate of declining Arctic sea ice appears ambiguous, leaving national governments to debate the needed level of concern over any increase in governance or security cooperation in the region.

The Arctic region is also rich in mineral resources under extraction. This includes the Red Dog Mine in Alaska, producing zinc and lead.[33] Arctic waters, particularly the Bering Sea

[28]National Snow and Ice Data Center, "A better year for the cryoshpere," www.nsidc.org, (Accessed March 9, 2014).

[29]Fox News, "Arctic sea ice up 60 percent in 2013," *Fox News*, September 09, 2013.

[30]Justin Gillis, "Arctic Ice Makes Comeback From Record Low, but Long-Term Decline May Continue," *The New York Times*, Environment, September 20, 2013.

[31]National Snow and Ice Data Center, "Ice thickness and age," in *A better year for the cryoshpere*, www.nsidc.org, (accessed March 9, 2014).

[32]Lisa Alexander et. al., "*Climate Change 2013: The Physical Science Basis*," SPM-17.

[33]NANA Regional Corporation, Inc., "Red Dog Operations," www.reddogalaska.com (accessed March 17, 2014).

within the 10-degree isotherm line, is a prosperous region for fisheries resources. The future transformation of the Arctic region involves the great potential of resources and the increased access to the region afforded by receding ice. Nations are taking notice of the increased opportunities and are already racing to stake competing claims over resource-rich areas.

Shipping Routes

Two seasonal waterways through the Arctic region are partially ice-free during the month of September and garner increased interest for their potential use for maritime commerce. The Northwest Passage (NWP) bears the same name as the famed passage sought by explorers for centuries. The NWP passes through the Canadian northern archipelago and through several narrow straits. The Northern Sea Route (NSR) is the famed Northeast Passage (NEP) that also eluded explorers. The route's nomenclature, often referred to by its old name of the Northeast Passage, is the Northern Sea Route in this study. The two shipping routes, depicted in figure 2, connect the Atlantic and Pacific Oceans, and can significantly reduce shipping distances from current maritime routes. The continued receding Arctic ice may open up a third passage even shorter than the NWP or NSR, the center red line in figure 2. This potential route would traverse the center of the Arctic across the North Pole. This route may not be open for any period of the year for decades according to scientific models.[34]

---

[34]Smith and Stephenson, "New Trans-Arctic shipping routes," E1191-E1195.

Figure 2: Map of the Arctic region depicting navigation routes correlating with the Northwest Passage, Northern Sea Route, and the potential transarctic route over the North Pole.

Source: Laurence C. Smith and Scott R. Stephenson, "New Trans-Arctic shipping routes navigable by midcentury," *Proceedings of the National Academy of Science of the United States of America*, vol. 110 no. 13 (2013): E1191-E1195.[35]

---

[35]Blue lines designate routes for common open-water (OW) ships. Red lines designate Polar Class 6 (PC6) ships with moderate ice-breaking capacity.

Economic Opportunities

In September 2007, satellite data showed the famed Northwest Passage route through the northern Canadian Archipelago and the Northern Sea Route across Russia's northern coast emerged as ice-free for the first time since satellite records began.[36] This opened the possibility for maritime traffic through the sea passage. Reportedly, up to 6,000 vessels operated in or near the Arctic region in 2004, according to the Arctic Council.[37] Four commercial vessels sailed through the NSR for the first time in 2010.[38] The reported number of vessels passing through the NSR in 2011 increased to 46 in 2012 during the ice-free months.[39] A large freighter, not configured for icebreaking, completed a voyage through the NWP in September 2013, showing the potential for greater use of the passage for commercial shipping. Estimates are that the freighter's journey through the NWP saved around $80,000 of fuel and cut a week from the traditional route through the Panama Canal. Observers of the Arctic region, and national governments took notice of these emerging economic opportunities.

---

[36]John Roach, "Arctic Melt Opens Northwest Passage," *National Geographic News*, September 17, 2007.

[37]L. Brigham, et al., ed., *Arctic Marine Shipping Assessment 2009 Report* (Reykjavik : Arctic Council, 2009), 72.

[38]Scott Borgerson, "The Coming Arctic Boom," *Foreign Affairs* (July/August 2013): 82.

[39]Ibid.

Figure 3: September 2007 mosaic image taken by European Space Agency satellites of Arctic sea ice. The melt has completely opened the Northwest Passage (yellow line) and mostly cleared the Northeast Passage (blue line).

Source: John Roach, "Arctic Melt Opens Northwest Passage," National Geographic News. September 17, 2007.

The neighboring nations of the Arctic created a multi-lateral group to help regulate and manage the future of the region. Known as the Arctic Council, it is a high-level intergovernmental forum for coordination and interaction among Arctic states. The Arctic Council dates its origins to the 1996 Ottawa Declaration.[40] The council's members are already studying and negotiating regulation of the Arctic region's activity and extention of international law. The *2009 Arctic Marine Shipping Assessment* (AMSA) was commissioned by the Arctic Council with findings on the future regulation of marine activity in the newly opened Arctic sea routes.[41] The AMSA anticipates an ice-free Arctic as early as 2015,[42] much earlier than the findings of the IPCC or the NSIDC. However, the new sea routes lack economic viability without marine infrastructure. The AMSA recognized the uncharted and ungoverned aspect of the Arctic routes making marine transport too dangerous for shipping. There are gaps in hydrographic data of the region for safe navigation. Unlike other oceans, the Arctic lacks proper oceanographic data, products and services, or information on sea ice and icebergs. Lacking such data increases the risk of a Titanic-like disaster. There is a lack of emergency response capacity for saving lives and mitigating pollution except for limited areas of the Arctic region. The AMSA includes several recommendations to improve the safety and maritime infrastructure of the Arctic that could enable more regional economic activity.[43]

Despite the recession of the polar ice, some experts believe that continuing ice floes, and continued extreme Arctic conditions would still prevent opening of the sea passages to greater maritime activity. Rather than a Arctic boom of commerce leaving international law and

[40]Arctic Council, *Declaration on the Establishment of the Arctic Council* (Ottawa: Arctic Council, 1996), 1-4.

[41]L. Brigham, et al., ed. "Arctic Marine Shipping Assessment 2009 Report," 2-5.

[42]Ibid., 4.

[43]Ibid., 5-7.

regulation slow to keep up, the changes are slow enough, and manageable by international agreement. The book *Arctic Security in the Age of Climate Change*, is composed of several essays on the security issues of the Arctic by several international experts.[44] Lawson W. Brigham of the University of Alaska Fairbanks comments on the assessment of the AMSA in the essay "The Challenges and Security Issues of Arctic Marine Transport." Brigham was also the lead author of the Arctic Council's AMSA report. He asserts that the opening of Arctic sea routes and improved regulation are slow enough to allow time for international regulation and reduced tension.[45] An ice-free Arctic in the future is not completely ice-free for economically viable shipping. Such future ice-free summers only exist for a few months of the year regardless of when in the twenty-first century the Arctic becomes ice-free. Masses of floating sea ice and icebergs would still block the new transport routes, making transport slow and unsafe.[46] Maritime traffic could still be restricted to special polar-class ships capable of breaking through ice, and prevent regular shipping to use the sea routes regularly. Any Arctic shipping may be slow and cautious, negating any benefit from shorter routes between markets.[47] The lack of infrastructure in the Arctic also impedes access by naval and other military forces to the region. The numerous variables potentially affecting a more open Arctic region to global shipping leaves much uncertainty. There are numerous unmet challenges that leave the question of if the region may be a future hotbed of international competition and lawlessness, or a quiet frontier kept stable by regulation or lack of viability for exploitation.

---

[44]James Kraska, ed., *Arctic Security in the Age of Climate Change* (New York: Cambridge, 2011).

[45]Lawson W. Brigham, "The Challenges and Security Issues of Arctic Marine Transport," in *Arctic Security in the Age of Climate Change*, ed., James Kraska (New York: Cambridge, 2011), 32.

[46]Ibid., 28-29.

[47]Ibid., 28-29.

Resources

The important actors expanding their interests in the Arctic believe that a vast, untapped,

wealth of resources lie beneath the receding ice. The United States Geological Survey (USGS)

conducted an appraisal of the possible future reserves of oil and natural gas in the Arctic region in

May 2008. The USGS scientists concluded that up to 90 billion barrels of oil, 1,669 trillion cubic

feet of natural gas, and 44 billion barrels of natural gas liquids might remain unexplored in the

Arctic. Approximately 84 percent of these potential resources might be in offshore areas affecting

maritime traffic. This total amounts to 13 percent of the world's undiscovered oil resources and

30 percent of undiscovered natural gas.[48]

Two of the indispensible Arctic nations, the United States and Russia, are realizing the

resources wealth just beyond their shores. Both seek to stake their claims with backing from

international law, or assertion of their perceived rights. Ariel Cohen of the Heritage Foundation

writes about the energy security stakes for the United States and Russia in the Arctic region, for

the Strategic Studies Institute (SSI). His essay on Arctic energy security, *Russia in the Arctic:*

Challenges to US Energy and Geopolitics in the High North, is part of the SSI book, *Russia in the*

Arctic. Cohen sees Arctic hydrocarbon wealth as key to the energy security of the United States

and Russia, and predicts a race for developing and exploiting such resources.[49] Cohen cites

America's USGS estimates of the potential resource wealth in the Arctic and the Russian

Ministry of Natural Resources estimate, which is up to 586 billion barrels of oil reserves and 88.3

trillion cubic meters of natural gas.[50] Cohen's assertion is that the United States must stake its

---

[48]Peter H. Stauffer, ed., *Circum-Arctic Resource Appraisal: Estimates of Undiscovered Oil and Gas North of the Arctic Circle* (Menlo Park: USGS, 2008), 1-4.

[49]Ariel Cohen, "Russia in the Arctic: Challenges to US Energy and Geopolitics in the High North," in *Russia in the Arctic*, ed., Stephen J. Blank (Carlisle: US Army War College, 2011), 1.

[50]Ibid., 3-4.

Arctic territorial claims as Alaska's Prudhoe Bay reserves are declining and world oil markets are uncertain.[51] Cohen advocates fulfilling US Arctic strategy as per the 2009 National Security Presidential Directive 66 (NSPD-66)[52] which states that the United States must "take all actions necessary to establish the outer limit of the continental shelf."[53] The United States may be falling short in securing its energy interests in the Arctic according to Cohen. The stakes for the United States is Russia's "hardened international posture," and stepped up, "anti-American policies and rhetoric," to challenge US interests. Russian aggressiveness was notable after Russia's 2008 invasion of Georgia.[54] Cohen cites Russia submitting claims for the disputed Lomonosov Ridge extending to the North Pole to the United Nations in 2001. The UN rejected the claim, which the Russians responded by planting an undersea flag on the ocean floor in 2007.[55] Russia's symbolic gestures and statements of, "the Arctic is ours,"[56] run counter to the spirit of international cooperation, according to Cohen. The essay, *Russia in the Arctic: Challenges to US Energy and Geopolitics in the High North*, infers, if not implies, a heightened potential of conflict in the Arctic between the United States and Russia over natural resources.

Some experts see the future Arctic as the next great commercial boom, with less concern for security issues and tension. Scott G. Borgerson, an International Affairs Fellow at the Council on Foreign Relations, sees the future exploitation of Arctic resources as a stable region with shared prosperity. His views on the Arctic evolved from alarmist and anticipating future conflict,

---

[51]Ibid., 5-6.

[52]Ibid., 11-12.

[53]George W. Bush, *National Security Presidential Directive and Homeland Security Presidential Directive 66* (Washington: The White House, 2009), 3.

[54]Cohen, "Russia in the Arctic," 14.

[55]Ibid., 14-16.

[56]Ibid., 15.

much like Cohen's essay, to an "Arctic Boom."[57] Mr. Borgerson wrote essays in *Foreign Affairs* Magazine in 2008, titled *Arctic Meltdown*,[58] and *The Great Game Moves North*.[59] Bold Russian claims, opening waterways, and estimates of large hydrocarbon reserves with lacking international regulation were cause for his concerns. Mr. Borgerson's recent 2013 article in *Foreign Affairs*, *The Coming Arctic Boom*, explains his reversal from alarmist to optimistic about exploitation of Arctic resources. He sees cooperative efforts by Arctic nations to manage disputes as avoiding the trend of "anarchy," or "armed brinksmanship," as he wrote in 2008 and 2009.[60] Now, the Arctic region is a promising economic boom of hydrocarbon, mineral riches, and other opportunities. For example, undersea telecommunications cables, made possible from receding ice; and data-storage centers, benefitting from cool temperatures; are among the possibilities of the future Arctic explored by companies like Facebook.[61]

Strategic Context of the Arctic Region

Within a decade nations could be at war over resources in the Arctic Ocean.
Russian national security strategy statement, May 2009[62]

Actors

The strategic actors affecting the present and future of the Arctic region are the littoral nations within the region; nations in the periphery of the Arctic, or sub-Arctic; outer nations increasing their interests in the Arctic region; and non-state actors including international

---

[57]Scott G. Borgerson, "The Coming Arctic Boom," *Foreign Affairs* (July/August 2013): 79-82.

[58]Borgerson, "Arctic Meltdown."

[59]Borgerson, Scott G., "The Great Game Moves North," *Foreign Affairs*, www.foreignaffairs.com (accessed April 16, 2014).

[60]Borgerson, "Arctic Meltdown," 4.

[61]Borgerson, "The Coming Arctic Boom," 79-82.

[62]Dmitry Medvedev, *National Security Strategy Russia 2020, Decree No. 537* (Moscow: Security Council of the Russian Federation, May 12, 2009).

regimes. Arctic nations include the five countries that border the Arctic Ocean. The "Arctic Five," includes Canada, Russia, United States (via Alaska), Denmark (via Greenland), and Norway. The Arctic Council counts a more inclusive group of states as Arctic nations. The Arctic Council is composed of the "Arctic Eight," the five Arctic maritime nations plus Sweden, Finland, and Iceland.[63] This study will use the Arctic Council standards and refer to the Arctic 8 as Arctic nations. Non-Arctic nations are countries that are not geographically in or near the Arctic region, but increase their activity in the region and extend their interests. The twelve states granted observer status within the Arctic Council are the non-Arctic states.[64] The People's Republic of China (PRC), granted observer status in May 2013, considers itself a "near-Arctic nation."[65] The Arctic Council definition of non-Arctic nation describes nations asserting interests in the Arctic, but otherwise not geographically related to the region.

The observations of state and non-state actors with interests in the Arctic region are as rational actors. This realist view draws from the theories of international relations of Kenneth N. Waltz and Stephen D. Krasner. Waltz's neorealist theory states that nations interact within a system of anarchy, lacking any strong international governance. Nations in the anarchic system create a balance behaving out of self-interest.[66] The theory applies to the interaction of the powerful Arctic and non-Arctic nations as they further their interests in the region. Krasner's International Regime theory applies to how international institutions or regimes affect the behavior of states and non-state agents.[67] International regimes affecting the Arctic region such as

---

[63] Arctic Council, "Member States," www.arctic-council.org (accessed November 8, 2013).

[64] Ibid., "Observers," (accessed November 8, 2013).

[65] Shiloh Rainwater, "Race to the North: China's Arctic Strategy and Its Implications" *Naval War College Review*, Spring 2013 (2013): 63.

[66] Kenneth N. Waltz, *Theory of International Politics* (Long Grove: Waveland, 1979), 102, 123-128.

[67] Stephen D. Krasner, "Structural causes and regime consequences: regimes as intervening

the Arctic Council, United Nations, UN Convention on the Law of the Sea (UNCLOS), and the North Atlantic Treaty Organization (NATO) are growing in significance in regulating the anarchic trends among Arctic nations and non-state actors.

Arctic Nations

The five Arctic nations - Russia, Canada, United States, Denmark, and Norway - are all increasing their exploration and assessing their security interests in the region. Russia and Canada own the most territory in the Arctic, both land and maritime, while controlling the NSR and NWP respectively. The big three Arctic nations of Russia, Canada, and the United States are among the richest and most powerful global nations. All have vast Arctic hydrocarbon and mineral resources under extraction or potentially exploited by energy companies. All are wary of each other at some level, even allies like Canada and the United States. The policies and strategies of the three large Arctic powers are of deep interest to the other two Arctic nations and the outer non-Arctic nations. As the littoral Arctic nations see threats to their self interests in the Arctic, their approaches towards each other may be more realist.

Russia

Russian approaches in the Arctic region are realist, securing its own self-interests. Russia abides by international law to suit its interests, they are a signatory to UNCLOS and formally submitted their Arctic territorial claims through the UN body. It was an act of Russian nationalism at the seabed of the North Pole that caused concern over Arctic security. In 2007, a Russian adventurer planted a flag at the seabed of the North Pole. The UNCLOS is the international regulatory framework for maritime claims, and defines the borders among the

---

variables," in *International Regimes*, ed. Stephen D. Krasner (Ithaca: Cornell University, 1983), 1-21.

littoral Arctic nations.[68] It was through the UNCLOS articles pertaining to expanded maritime areas, or Exclusive Economic Zones (EEZ), that Russia staked its expanded claim of Arctic waters in 2001.[69] UNCLOS allows maritime nations an EEZ of 200 nautical miles from their territorial sea. An EEZ can extend beyond this limit if the continental shelf is further than 200 nautical miles.[70] Russia claimed that the Lomonosov Ridge near the North Pole was an extension of their continental shelf. The UN rejected the claim. If approved, the claim potentially extended Russian territory and its resources to an area of 1.2 million square kilometers, or 460,000 square miles. Russian claims extended over the North Pole.[71] Russia continues to assert this claim in dispute with Canada and Denmark.[72] Russia currently behaves cooperatively and relies on international law to gain recognition of its stake to Arctic territory. Other aggressive Russian behavior towards its neighbors, such as Georgia in 2008, and Ukraine in 2014 raise alarms about what Russia may do if it's Arctic claims are frustrated.

Some Russian experts see the Arctic region as an area that may see more Russian aggressiveness. In *Russia in the Arctic*, a series of essays by Russian foreign policy experts by the US Army's Strategic Studies Institute, examines Russian approaches towards its neighbors and plans to assert dominance in the region.[73] Experts on international law also examine Russian Arctic intentions through essays in *Arctic Security in the Age of Climate Change*.[74] An idea of the

---

[68]United Nations, "United Nations Convention on the Law of the Sea (UNCLOS)," www.un.org (accessed March 18, 2014).

[69]Cohen, "Russia in the Arctic," 14-15.

[70]United Nations, "UNCLOS, Part V, Exclusive Economic Zone," www.un.org (accessed March 18, 2014) Article 57.

[71]Cohen, "Russia in the Arctic," 14-15.

[72]Alistair MacDonald, "Canada Set to Stake Claim on North Pole, But Not Quite Yet," *Wall Street Journal*, December 9, 2013.

[73]Blank, ed., *Russia in the Arctic*.

[74]Kraska, ed., *Arctic Security in the Age of Climate Change*.

Russian point of view, particularly fears of perceived threats from the United States, its allies, and NATO, is revealed in an article by a Russian military officer in the Russian military journal, *Military Thought, a Theoretical Journal of the Russian General Staff.*[75]

Ariel Cohen, in *Russia in the Arctic*, notes that Russian assertiveness in the Arctic extended beyond formal territorial claims and symbolic gestures, but in their stated national strategies. Dmitry Medvedev, the Russian President in 2009, released an Arctic strategy for Russia in May of that year. The strategy anticipated the potential for conflicts over resources in the Arctic Ocean.[76] In preparation, the strategy allowed the increase of commercial activity in Russia's claimed Arctic territory. The Russian Arctic strategy called for new development and exploration of hydrocarbon reserves. Russia began construction of nuclear power stations to support oil and natural gas projects as well as building new polar icebreaker ships for increased accessibility.[77]

Alexandr' Golts, the defense correspondent for Yezhenedevnyi Zhurnal (Daily Journal), and Marlene Laruelle of the Central Asia-Caucasus Institute, contribute in *Russia in the Arctic* on Russia's growing militarization of the Arctic region. Golts's essay, *The Arctic: A Clash of Interests or Clash of Ambitions*, noted how Russia's 2008 strategy expands naval, air, and ground forces into the Arctic as well as extended intelligence gathering and FSB forces, Russia's security and intelligence agency, to protect borders.[78] The implementation of these policies occurred with assertive military actions such as a symbolic landing of airborne troops at the North Pole and flights by bombers into Canadian airspace in 2009. The Canadian military scrambled fighters,

---

[75]A. Yu. Maruyev, Col., "Russia and the USA in Confrontation: Military and Political Aspects," *Military Thought, Monthly Theoretical Journal of the Russian General Staff* (2013): 2

[76]Cohen, "Russia in the Arctic," 19-21.

[77]Ibid., 21-25.

[78]Alexandr' Golts, "The Arctic: A Clash of Interests or Clash of Ambitions," in *Russia in the Arctic*, ed., Stephen J. Blank. (Carlisle: US Army War College, 2011), 46.

after detection by North American Air Defense (NORAD) radar, to intercept the Russian bombers.[79] Marlene Laruelle's essay in SSI, *Russian Military Presence in the High North: Projection of Power and Capacities of Action*, notes the same military build-up and activities by the Russians. However, her more measured analysis is that Russia's militarization is pragmatic attempts to reform and modernize its military forces.[80]

Caitlyn L. Antrim, the executive director of the Rule of Law Committee for the Oceans, and leading expert on the US experience with the UNCLOS, sees Russia's increased activity in the Arctic as a natural geographical pivot to gain better access to world markets. *In The Arctic in Twentieth-Century Geopolitics*, an essay in *Arctic Security in the Age of Climate Change*, Antrim sees Russia's Arctic coast as a "fourth wall" of containment that historically kept its power in check during the Cold War.[81] She cites the geopolitical theories of Alfred Thayer Mahan and Halford J. Mackinder from the turn of the twentieth century, viewing Russia as naturally expanding through its opening northern coast as it faces obstacles along its other borders in Eurasia. Both Mahan and Mackinder recognized the geographical needs for great powers to gain access to key ports and global trade through the oceans. Russia's encroachments into the Arctic, both commercial and military, are allowing the opportunities of ocean access afforded by the warming Arctic region.[82] Antrim assesses that Russia sees itself as a dominant Arctic power. The nationalist narrative Russia promotes is of a dominant Arctic power. This is demonstrated by

---

[79]Ibid., 44.

[80]Marlene Laruelle, "Russian Military Presence in the High North: Projection of Power and Capacities of Action," in *Russia in the Arctic*, ed., Stephen J. Blank (Carlisle: US Army War College, 2011), 67.

[81]Caitlyn L. Antrim, "The Arctic in Twentieth-Century Geopolitics," in *Arctic Security in the Age of Climate Change*, ed., James Kraska (New York: Cambridge, 2011), 110.

[82]Ibid., 108-111.

Russian rhetoric and assertiveness in its northern territories.[83] President Vladimir Putin, who continues to dominate Russian politics, furthers Russian nationalist ideals of the Arctic.

The Russian point of view on Arctic security is negative toward the United States, NATO, and the west in general. Colonel A. Tu. Maruyev of the Russian military, wrote a research paper in *Military Thought, a Theoretical Journal of the Russian General Staff*. Titled, *Russia and the USA in Confrontation: Military and Political Aspects*, Maruyev's paper views the United States and its Atlantic allies as Russia's principal "geopolitical enemy," intent on weakening Russia's power.[84] He asserts that the United States foreign policy is furthering a strategy of achieving "global supremacy."[85] Protecting Russia's border and claims in the Arctic with a stronger military presence is important to fending off American encroachment. Maruyev disputes any resistance to Russian territorial claims. The United States and Norway, as its Atlantic ally, are the two greatest threats to Arctic interests, monitored by a wary Russia.[86]

Canada

Canada considers itself a key Arctic power with its own vast coastline and natural resources in the region. The northern nation generally considers its foreign policy posture as liberal, as it espouses human rights and international law.[87] Canada increasingly becomes more realist in its approach in securing its self interests in the Arctic region, however, its own interests in the north waxed and waned through the country's history. Canada's Arctic interests and activity increased at times with the discovery of mineral and hydrocarbon resources. Currently,

---

[83]Ibid., 120-122.

[84]Maruyev, "Russia and the USA in Confrontation," 2.

[85]Ibid., 2.

[86]Ibid., 10.

[87]Government of Canada, "Canada's Foreign Policy," www.international.gc.ca (accessed on April 16, 2014).

the Canadian Arctic oil sands produce up to 170 billion barrels of oil, and additional oil may be under the Beaufort Sea in the Arctic. [88] Periods of increased military interest coincided with US military interest in the Arctic. In World War II, Canada permitted the United States to construct military facilities and the Alaska-Canada highway through their northwest to defend against the Japanese Empire. Through the Cold War, the United States regarded Canada as key to a greater North American defense.[89] The two nations established the North American Aerospace Defense Command (NORAD) in 1957 to protect against an approaching Soviet nuclear attack over the North Pole.[90] Canadian interests in the Arctic are increasing again in response to the emerging opportunities of climate change and other Arctic nations' rising activity.

Canada's foreign policy approach in the Arctic and how it sees its security interests in the region are examined through articles and books by notable Canadian academics and military officers. Canadian armed forces officers, Major Daniel R. Bobbitt, Major Sonny Hatton, and Major Tony Balasevicius, each have differing views of Canada's best approach to viewing its neighbors and securing its Arctic interests. Major Bobbitt wrote a SAMS monograph on Canada's published national strategy in the Arctic, criticizing its dated "Cold War mentality."[91] Major Hatton's SAMS monograph looks into Canadian unilateralism in securing its Arctic interests.[92] Major Balasevicius's article in the Canadian military journal, is the more realist of the military officers. He lists the the United States as a threat to Canada's Arctic interests.[93] The Canadian

---

[88]Alberta Energy, "Facts and Statistics," www.energy.alberta.ca (accessed March 19, 2014).

[89]Daniel R. Bobbitt, MAJOR, Canadian Armed Forces, "Canada's 2009 Northern Strategy: Cold War Policy in a Warming Arctic" (Monograph, School of Advanced Military Studies, 2010), 15.

[90]North American Aerospace Defense Command, "NORAD Agreement," www.norad.mil (Accessed March 19, 2014).

[91]Bobbitt, "Canada's 2009 Northern Strategy."

[92]Hatton, "Canadian Unilateralism in the Arctic"

[93]Tony Balasevicius, "Towards a Canadian Forces Arctic Operating Concept," *Canadian Military*

legal scholar, and expert on international law, Michael Byers, seeks approaches for Canada to resolve disputes with its neighbor, the United States.[94] Finally, Whitney Lackenbauer notes Canada's "bi-polar view" of the United States as threat and ally.[95]

On February 18, 2009, two Russian Tupolev TU-95 bombers approached Canadian airspace, and turned away when met by Canadian forces CF-18 fighters over the Beaufort Sea. The Russian bombers did not enter Canadian territory, but the incident sparked renewed Canadian attention to protecting its own Arctic sovereignty. This generated concerns of increased tension by international experts in the region. The Canadian Prime Minister, Stephen Harper, stated in response to the incident his concerns about "increasingly aggressive Russian actions" and "intrusion into our airspace."[96] The same year, Canada released its Northern Strategy, stating the country's interests and goals in the region. The strategy declared Canada's priorities of "exercising Arctic sovereignty" by "putting more boots on the Arctic tundra, more ships in the icy water, and a better eye-in-the-sky."[97] Canada's increased military presence in the Arctic included significant investments in an army training center, expanding and modernizing the Canadian Rangers, a new coast guard polar icebreaker, new navy patrol ships, and better monitoring capabilities to observe the maritime boundary and NWP. Canadian forces also conduct the Operation NANOOK annual training exercises in the Arctic with international participants to include the US Navy.[98]

Journal, (Spring 2011): 25.

[94]Byers, *Who Owns the Arctic?*

[95]Lackenbauer, Whitney, PhD,

[96]Ibid., Kindle Electronic Edition, Location, 106-118.

[97]Government of Canada, *Canada's Northern Strategy, Our North, Our Heritage, Our Future*, (Ottawa: Government of Canada, 2009), 9.

[98]Ibid., 10-11.

Canadian sovereignty concerns in the Arctic includes wariness of the United States along with concerns over Russian assertiveness in the Arctic. Major Daniel R. Bobbitt of the Canadian Armed Forces, and graduate of the US Army School of Advanced Military Studies (SAMS), wrote a monograph on Canada's 2009 Northern Strategy. In his monograph, Bobbitt criticized Canada's strategy for being more appropriate to the Cold War than to current realities.[99] Bobbitt describes Canada's Cold War mentality as perceiving the United States as its principal threat.[100] Writing in *Arctic Security in the Age of Climate Change*, P. Whitney Lackenbauer of St. Jeromes University in Ontario also notes the bi-polar view of Canada toward its southern neighbor.[101] Canada's concern about United States encroachment of its sovereignty dated back to World War II. The belief, then, was that the United States would maintain a permanent military presence in Canada after the war.[102] This proved unfounded as the US military departed after the Japanese surrender. Canadian fears renewed with the military cooperation with the United States in the Cold War. As both nations built the Distant Early Warning (DEW) Line and established NORAD, Canadian public opinion and the media saw an "abrogation of sovereignty."[103] According to Major Bobbitt on current Canadian opinion, "few now seriously argue that the United States harbored territorial ambitions over Canada's Arctic."[104] A 2011 article in the *Canadian Military Journal* by Major Tony Balasevicius of the Canadian Armed Forces, expresses concerns of increased US military activity in the Arctic. The article notes the activities of the US Navy fleet operations and Russian bomber flights, such as the 2009 event, as a source of ongoing tensions in

---

[99]Bobbitt, "Canada's 2009 Northern Strategy," 3, 53.

[100]Ibid., 44.

[101]Lackenbauer, *Arctic Security in the Age of Climate Change*.

[102]Ibid.

[103]Bobbitt, "Canada's Northern Strategy," 19

[104]Ibid., 44, 45.

the region. Balasevicius also describes the territorial disputes with the United States over the maritime border with Alaska over the Beaufort Sea, and ownership of the NWP. The US position on the NWP and NSR is that they are international routes. Canada asserts that the NWP is an internal route, and maritime traffic is subject to their permission and regulation.[105]

Canadian wariness of neighbors includes an ongoing dispute with Denmark over Hans Island between Greenland and Canada's Northern Archipelago. Michael Byers writes in *Who Owns the Arctic? Understanding Sovereignty Disputes in the North*, that Canada resolve current Arctic tensions through cooperation with the United States, Russia, and other neighbors.[106] One of the most important adjudications of disputes, according to Byers, is an agreement with the United States over the NWP. Both countries have agreements on monitoring and securing the route through NORAD.[107] Byers asserts that the United States and Canada must negotiate a bi-lateral agreement reconciling Canadian sovereignty and US policy of freedom of the seas.[108] Such an agreement must include convincing the United States to also recognize Canadian claims to the NWP.[109]

In December 2013, Canada filed data with the UN defining the extent of its own continental shelf beyond the 200 nautical mile limit of the UNCLOS. Claiming that Canadian scientists proved the size of the continental shelf off the Canadian coast, the Government of Canada submitted a territorial claim that includes the North Pole. This disputes Russia's 2001 claim that also extended to the North Pole. The claim may take up to two years for the

---

[105]Balasevicius, "Towards a Canadian Forces Arctic Operating Concept," 25.

[106]Byers, *Who Owns the Arctic?*, Kindle Electronic Edition, Location, 1891-1909.

[107]Ibid., Loc. 959.

[108]Ibid., Loc. 1205.

[109]Ibid., Loc. 1215.

international arbitration process to approve.[110] Like Russia's 2001 claim, Canada's claim over Arctic territory may face rejection.

Major Sonny Hatton, another Canadian Armed Forces SAMS graduate, wrote on Canada's ability to act unilaterally in securing its sovereignty in the Arctic. With detailed analysis and case studies, his monograph, "Canadian Unilateralism in the Arctic: Using Scenario Planning to Help Canada Achieve its Strategic Goals in the North," concluded that Canada must work bi-laterally with the United States and through NATO to secure its sovereignty against a military threat.[111] The continued potential for Arctic conflict may force Canadian cooperation with the United States or risk a "major loss of sovereignty" if the United States decides to act unilaterally to secure its northern interests.[112] Canadian Arctic sovereignty is paramount to its strategy in the north. Canada faces numerous challenges of increasing its Arctic activities, both economic and military, while understanding its threats and ally's intentions.

United States

> "I believe in the future, whoever holds Alaska will hold the world. I think it is the most important strategic place in the world."
> - Brigadier General William "Billy" Mitchell, US Army Air Service[113]

The United States first expanded to the Arctic with the purchase of the Alaska territory from Russia in 1867.[114] America since became a key Arctic power, whether its attention to the region waxed or waned over 146 years. The stakes for US Arctic presence were first expansion as

---

[110]MacDonald, "Canada Set to Stake Claim on North Pole."

[111]Hatton, "Canadian Unilateralism in the Arctic," 72.

[112]Ibid., 73.

[113]Michael B. Rickard, Lt. Col., USAF, "US Arctic Security" (Research paper, Fletcher School, Tufts University, 2012), 7.

[114]Jonathan M. Nielson, *Armed Forces on a Northern Frontier: The Military in Alaska's History, 1867-1987* (Westport: Praeger, 1988), 5.

Alaska's population grew to achieve statehood in 1959.[115] The Arctic's economic importance grew with Alaska's strategic location for commercial air traffic and the development of the Prudhoe Bay oil fields on Alaska's north coast.[116] American security in the Arctic gained attention with wars in the twentieth century. Alaska's transportation infrastructure linking it with the 48 contiguous states and defenses increased in the 1930s in anticipation of the Pacific War against Imperial Japan.[117] The preparations paid off when U.S forces repulsed a Japanese invasion in the Aleutian Islands Campaign in 1942 and 1943.[118] Arctic security came to the fore again during the Cold War from 1947 to 1989. The North Pole was a potential nuclear front line between the United States and the Soviet Union in the event of war. The Arctic became an anticipated air avenue of approach for nuclear bombers and inter-continental ballistic missiles (ICBM). This threat prompted the United States to build the DEW Line of radar stations across the Alaskan north coast and the Canadian far north to detect incoming Soviet bombers.[119] Both the United States and Canada further strengthened security over the Arctic against the Soviet threat. The two nations established the NORAD in 1957.[120] The US security concerns in the Arctic decreased after the end of the Cold War, although NORAD continues to operate.[121]

Regarded as America's "Gibraltar of the North,"[122] Alaska's size and unique geography allow extensive operational reach for the US military and commercial logistics. The narrow

---

[115]Ibid., 179-180.

[116]Dermot Cole, *North to the Future: The Alaska Story, 1959-2009* (Kenmore: Epicenter, 2008) 137-143.

[117]Nielson, *Armed Forces on a Northern Frontier*, 125, 137-139.

[118]Ibid., 141, 159-168.

[119]Ibid., 187-189.

[120]North American Aerospace Defense Command, "About NORAD: NORAD Agreement," www.norad.mil (Accessed November 8, 2013).

[121]Ibid., NORAD History.

[122]Nielson, *Armed Forces on a Northern Frontier*, 179.

Bering Strait between Alaska and the Russian Far East may become key to controlling access to the NWP and NSR. Long considered vital to the defense of North America, military bases enabled Alaska to meet challenges in World War II and the Cold War.[123] Alaskan-based forces are also important to operational reach in the Asia-Pacific regions. The four active duty brigades under US Army Alaska (USARAK) include engineer, Stryker, airborne, and aviation units.[124] US air forces in Alaska includes advanced F-22 Raptor figher aircraft.[125] Alaska is key to strategic ballistic missile defense and early warning detection. The changes in the Arctic region and its growing strategic importance heighten Alaska's importance to projecting US forces and influence.[126]

US approaches to the Arctic region shows periods of militarization when faced with threats to its northern front, and especially, its sovereign territory of Alaska.[127] America's distinct interests in the Arctic region lead to approaches that may differ from general patterns of US foreign policy. The United States, still regarded as a superpower, upholds international law and works as a diplomatic power broker when mitigating international disputes.[128] This approach is seen in the US policy in the Arctic with its involvement in the Arctic Council, and upholding the tenets of the UNCLOS.[129] US views of international access to the Arctic dispute with Canadian sovereignty claims. The United States and Canada remain at odds over access to the NWP. The

---

[123]Ibid., 139-146, 181-189.

[124]US Army Alaska, "USARAK Organizations," www.usarak.army.mil (accessed March 26, 2014).

[125]447th Fighter Group, "Arctic Reserve Units," www.477fg.afrc.af.mil (accessed March 26, 2014).

[126]John H. Pendleton, *Arctic Capabilities* (Washington, DC: Government Accountability Office, 2012), 7-8.

[127]Nielson, *Armed Forces on a Northern Frontier*, 125, 137-139, 187-189.

[128]The White House, President Barack Obama, *National Strategy for the Arctic Region* (Washington, DC: The White House, 2013), 2.

[129]Ibid.

United States asserts the passage is an international waterway, while Canada asserts that it is sovereign maritime territory.[130] In March 2010, the then US Secretary of State, Hillary Clinton, rebuked Canada for excluding 3 of the Arctic 8 nations – Sweden, Finland, and Iceland – from a high-level Arctic Council meeting.[131] The US government still has its own issues of sovereignty over international law. Parts of the US Congress continue to block ratification of UNCLOS.[132]

The recent history of American militarization of its Arctic territory, Alaska, reveals the important relationship of the United States to the region and its enduring strategic interests. Jonathan M. Nielson and Dermot Cole note the United States's twentieth century military history in the Arctic in *Armed Forces on a Northern Frontier: The Military in Alaska's History, 1867-1987,*[133] and, *North to the Future: The Alaska Story, 1959-2009.*[134] Both include the numerous threats and challenges faced by the United States when defending its northern borders. Cohen's essay in SSI's *Russia in the Arctic*, reiterates United States stakes for securing the Arctic.[135] Recent reports from the Congressional Research Service (CRS) further the argument of increased United States involvement in shaping the near future of the Arctic region as an internationally equitable and peaceful region.[136]

The increased interest by Arctic nations over the region in 2007 and 2008 also spurred calls for US leadership and protection of its own claims. United States concerns in keeping pace

---

[130]Byers, *Who Owns the Arctic?,* Kindle Electronic Edition, Location, 1891-1909.

[131]Mary Beth Sheridan, "Clinton rebukes Canada at Arctic meeting," *Washington Post*, March 30, 2010.

[132]Thomas Wright, "Outlaw of the Sea," *Foreign Affairs*, August 7, 2012.

[133]Nielson, *Armed Forces on a Northern Frontier*, 5.

[134]Cole, *North to the Future,* 137-143.

[135]Cohen, "Russia in the Arctic," 11.

[136]Ronald O'Rourke, *Changes in the Arctic: Background and Issues for Congress* (Washington, DC: Government Accountability Office, 2011), 6-7.

with other Arctic nations is in its failure to ratify the UNCLOS agreement. Since the United States is a non-signatory to the UNCLOS. The concern is that the United States cannot submit territorial claims onto the continental shelf as Russia did in 2001.[137] The other four Arctic nations are signatories to the UNCLOS. Despite bi-partisan support, and strong advocacy from the Defense and State Departments, ratification of UNCLOS in Congress continues to be blocked.[138] Cohen noted that the United States asserts its Arctic claims onto its continental shelf in part as an independent sovereign nation separate from the UNCLOS. President Harry S. Truman's Proclamation No. 2667 allows the United States to stake its claims as an "independent sovereign nation," declaring that any hydrocarbon or other resources discovered beneath the US continental shelf are the property of the United States.[139] This would be an act of unilateralism by the United States in Arctic claims favoring a pre-UNCLOS presidential declaration over international law.

The United States Government first published a strategy towards the Arctic region in 2009. President George W. Bush's administration released National Security Policy Directive 66 (NSDP 66), *Arctic Region Policy*, in January 2009 as the strategy of the United States in the Arctic. It stressed ratification of the UNCLOS by Congress. The policy asserts that "the United States has broad and fundamental national security interests in the Arctic region and is prepared to operate either independently or in conjunction with other states to safeguard these interests."[140] In May 2013, President Barack Obama's administration released the *National Strategy for the Arctic Region*, with a more multi-lateral tone. The 2013 strategy states that "the United States is an Arctic Nation with broad and fundamental interests in the Arctic Region, where we seek to

---

[137]Ibid.

[138]Wright, "Outlaw of the Sea."

[139]Cohen, "Russia in the Arctic," 11.

[140]George W. Bush, "National Security Presidential Directive and Homeland Security Presidential Directive 66," 2-3.

33

meet our national security needs, protect the environment, responsibly manage resources, account for indigenous communities, support scientific research, and strengthen international cooperation on a wide range of issues."[141] In advancing security interests and safeguarding peace and stability, US strategy in the Arctic asserts the ability of vessels and aircraft to operate in the region, consistent with international law. The strategy also called for evolving Arctic infrastructure and capabilities, such as ice-capable platforms. The United States strategic approach will be informed by the guiding principles of maintaining and preserving the Arctic region as "free of conflict," and preserving freedom of navigation and over flight for all nations.[142]

The principle of keeping the Arctic an international region with freedom of access for all is the basis for working toward accession of the UNCLOS by the United States. Freedom of access is also the motivation for the United States declaring the NWP and NSR as international routes. This disputes with sovereignty claims by Canada and Russia over the two emerging waterways. The United States is also in dispute over maritime boundaries with Canada in the Beaufort Sea, and Russia in the Bering Sea where a signed boundary agreement is awaiting Russian ratification.[143]

---

[141]The White House, *National Strategy for the Arctic Region*, 2.

[142]Ibid., 2, 6.

[143]See figure 4.

Figure 4: Map of the Arctic depicting territorial claims. Four of the five Arctic nations stake claims beyond their 200 nautical mile limit into international waters.[144]
Source: Rajesh Mirchandani, "The struggle for Arctic riches," BBC News, www.bbc.co.uk (Accessed December 12, 2013).

---

[144]Russia submitted its claim to the UN in 2001, subsequently rejected. Canada submitted a territorial claim to the UN in December 2013, awaiting approval. Other Arctic international disputes include the United States/Russian border awaiting Russian parliamentary ratification; United States/Canadian border and freedom of use of the NWP; Canada/Denmark dispute over Hans Island, located in the narrow strait between the Canadian Archipelago and northwest Greenland.

Non-Arctic Nations

> After the Northwest Passage is opened up it will become a new 'axial sea route between the Atlantic and Pacific,' and the sea route between Europe, Asia, and North America will be shortened by 5,200 to 7,000 nautical miles. Whoever controls the Arctic sea route will control the world economy and a new internationally strategic corridor.
>
> Li Zhenfu, Dalian Maritime University[145]

> The Arctic belongs to all the people around the world, as no nation has sovereignty over it.... China must plan an indispensable role in Arctic exploration as we have one-fifth of the world's population.
>
> Rear Admiral Yin Zhuo, March 2010 Arctic Council meeting[146]

The three nations near the Arctic - Finland, Iceland, and Sweden - complete the Arctic 8 of the members of the Arctic Council. The three Arctic countries are non-Arctic nations in name only as they hold permanent participation status in the Arctic Council. The outer Arctic nations are highly involved in Arctic issues of security, climate, and indigenous issues of the region.[147] The Arctic region not only holds the interests of the Arctic 8, and the Arctic Council - non-Arctic nations, geographically distant from the Arctic Circle, are likewise seeking to increase their activity and exploit the opportunities of the region. According to the Arctic expert, Oran R. Young, in *Arctic Security in the Age of Climate change*, several non-Arctic nations are already highly involved in the region, and want to expand. India, Italy, the European Union, Japan, South Korea, Singapore, and China all want to engage in the economic opportunities of the Arctic region. These non-Arctic nations seek to increase their participation in fishing, commercial shipping through the passages, and natural resource exploitation.[148] These Arctic-interested nations gained admittance to the Arctic Council as observers. The EU could not apply as one

---

[145]David Curtis Wright, *Panda Bear Readies to Meet Polar Bear* (Calgary: Canadian Defense and Foreign Affairs Institute, 2011), 1.

[146]David Curtis Wright, *The Dragon Eyes the Top of the World* (Newport: US Naval War College, 2011), 2.

[147]Arctic Council, "Member States," www.arctic-council.org (accessed March 27, 2014).

[148]Oran R. Young, forward to *Arctic Security in the Age of Climate Change*, ed., James Kraska (New York: Cambridge, 2011), xxiv-xxv.

entity; instead, each European country applied for observer status independently.[149] The UNCLOS agreement pertains to all maritime nations and allows such non-Arctic nations the right to participate in the economic activities of the Arctic region. Many, such as China and the EU nations, are powerful global nations economically and militarily. These wealthy nations have much to offer to Arctic nations in capital and capability to collaborate on exploiting natural resources. Russia is cultivating relationships with members of the EU, China, and India. Some of the more powerful non-Arctic nations such as China and EU nations may not be content with permanent observer status in the council as their own interests increase in the region. China is an emergent global power extending its influence and economic interests among its neighbors and abroad, and the Arctic region is a coveted frontier.

China

The People's Republic of China (PRC) continues to expand its interests across the globe to support its growing economy. The emergent Asian nation's economic growth averaged around 10% over the past 3 decades and is anticipated to continue to grow.[150] This growth prompts China to extend its interests to other continents such as Africa, South America, and Australia. The PRC's particular interests are in gaining hydrocarbon resources to sustain its economic growth. Views on China's foreign policy is of realism. The PRC seeks to secure its self-interests, ensuring its continued economic growth, and preserving the Communist party's power. These self-interests may extend to securing the resource wealth of the Arctic region.

---

[149]Arctic Council, "Observers," www.arctic-council.org (accessed March 27, 2014).

[150]International Monetary Fund, "World Economic Outlook Database, April 2013, China," www.imf.org (accessed March 27, 2014).

Chinese Arctic interests already increased, first with its foothold of gaining observer status in the Arctic Council in May 2013.[151] Much of China's economic activity is with its sub-Arctic investments in resource extraction in the Russian Far East.[152] The PRC is seeking to increase its own accessibility to the Arctic region, particularly through the passages, with the construction of its own polar icebreaking ships. The *Xue Long*, or Snow Dragon, is the only Chinese icebreaking ship in service with a second one under construction expected to enter service in 2014.[153] Chinese interests in the Arctic, like most other nations, previously were in exploration and scientific research. Since 2004, China maintains a permanent land presence with its Arctic Yellow River Research Station in the Svalbard Archipelago.[154] The non-Arctic nation's observer status on the Arctic Council allows it a place at council meetings, proposing projects, and financing with limits.[155] China does not have a stated Arctic strategy document like many of the Arctic nations. Through the council and its permanent member status on the UN, China states its position that the Arctic Ocean and waterways must remain international territory.[156] Deductions of Chinese strategy regarding the Arctic are from its statements and academic articles on the subject. The PRC wants to partake in the potential resource wealth of the Arctic for its

---

[151]Steven Lee Myers, "Arctic Council Adds 6 Nations as Observer States, Including China," *New York Times*, May 15, 2013.

[152]Gabe Collins, "China Looms Over Russian Far East," *The Diplomat*, East Asia/Security/China, June 22, 2011.

[153]Michael J. Cole, "China to build second icebreaker for Arctic expeditions," *Jane's Navy International 2011* (September 2011): 1.

[154]Chinese Arctic and Antarctic Administration, "Chinese Arctic Yellow River Station," www.chinare.gov.cn (accessed March 27, 2014).

[155]Arctic Council, "Observers," www.arctic-council.org (accessed March 27, 2014).

[156]Wright, *The Dragon Eyes the Top of the World,* 10.

growing economy. Its position is allowing international access, and denying the Arctic nations' claims to "carve up the Arctic for themselves."[157]

A literature review of Chinese academic writing regarding China's approach towards the Arctic reveals the Asian power's view on its place in the region. David Curtis Wright of the University of Calgary wrote assessments of Chinese approaches to the Arctic region based on studying the leading Chinese scholars and policymakers on the topic. First, in *The Dragon Eyes the Top of the World,* for the US Naval War College, Wright notes how Chinese legal scholars advocate an approach similar to the United States, asserting that the Arctic belongs to the international community.[158] This, according to Wright, allows China to stake Arctic claims with the same entitlement as the Arctic littoral nations. In *The Panda Bear Readies to meet the Polar Bear*, Wright assesses for the Canadian Defence and Foreign Affairs Institute on how China's Arctic approach may dispute with Canadian sovereignty claims and security.[159]

Wright, in *The Dragon Eyes the Top of the World*, assesses that China will respect the integrity of the 200 nautical mile limits of each Arctic nations' EEZ, but oppose or dispute any extended claims onto the continental shelf.[160] This puts Chinese foreign policy in the Arctic in line with the liberal views of the United States and other non-Arctic nations of the EU, while disputing the realist positions of Russia or Canada. Like the United States and the EU, China wants to maintain the freedom to benefit from the economic opportunities of the open waterways and resources. Wright's literature review on Chinese academic and legal study of Arctic sovereignty derives Chinese views on China's place in the region. Without a stated Arctic policy,

---

[157]Ibid., 10.

[158]Ibid., 10.

[159]Wright, *Panda Bear Readies to Meet Polar Bear,* 5-10.

[160]Ibid.

Chinese academics debate over sovereignty claims by Arctic states. They point out how historical possession is ill defined by the UNCLOS or the 1958 Geneva Convention. This, they assert, weakens sovereignty claims by Russia and Canada allowing freedom of access for nations like China.[161] This position of freedom of access in the Arctic contradicts China's own aggressive claims of sovereignty in the South China Sea. The Chinese academic, Li Zhenfu, of Dalian Maritime University states that China can stake Arctic territorial claims if they see territorial claims by littoral Arctic states as aggressive. He views Canadian claims to territory, such as the NWP, as legally weak with poorly defined standards of sovereignty.[162]

Wright wrote about emerging legal views of Chinese academia versus Canadian sovereignty in, *The Panda Bear Readies to Meet the Polar Bear*. Wright points out more Chinese study on the Arctic and indications of Chinese Arctic interests for the other Arctic actors. In, *The Dragon Eyes the Top of the World: Arctic Policy Debate and Discussion in China*, Wright examines the implications of Chinese Arctic interest for the Arctic nations. He believes that the Chinese are deeply interested in the opportunities of the Arctic and are concerned about missing out on their own claims to the region from other powers.[163] China considers itself an Arctic power equal to Russia, Canada, or the United States. China appears "reluctant to acknowledge that it being a non-Arctic country, its influence in the Arctic and Arctic affairs might be somewhat limited."[164] China may appear outwardly diplomatic, showing support for Arctic nations' sovereignty rights and freedom of access. The Chinese "nightmare scenario" is that the Arctic nations would seize the resource wealth of the Arctic to the exclusion of other nations. The most

---

[161]Ibid., 9-10.

[162]Ibid., 5-6.

[163]Wright, *Dragon Eyes the Top of the World*, 10-11.

[164]Ibid., 10.

emotional language used by Chinese scholars on Arctic issues is the description of the Arctic

Council's Arctic 8 nations as the, "Eight-State Polar Regional Alliance." This term was evocative

of the "Eight-State Allied Forces" – western nations that sacked Beijing in the aftermath of the

Boxer Rebellion in 1900. Such reminders of China's century of humiliation through the

nineteenth and twentieth centuries are to create urgency for Chinese intervention in Arctic

affairs.[165] The academic, Li Zhengfu, of the Dalian Maritime University, is very aware of the

changes in the Arctic region and the opportunities of the opening waterways and resource wealth.

He strongly advocates that China immediately increase its role in the Arctic and expand

commercial activity to use the passages and claim hydrocarbon resources. This includes the

building of more Arctic-capable vessels to navigate the NWP and NSR, and oil and natural gas

tankers. Li stresses China's need to assert itself into Arctic issues with negotiating with the Arctic

nations and the UNCLOS. China could then attain rights to the wealth of the Arctic for its own

interests.[166]

There is not a clear Arctic strategy from the Chinese government despite the advocacy of

its academics. A 2013 white paper on the employment of China's armed forces focused mostly on

the Chinese military's role in protecting local sovereignty. The paper did acknowledge China's

inclusion to the world economy and security. However, the white paper does not mention the

Arctic region, or Chinese interests in the Arctic. The Chinese armed forces recognize China's

growing inclusion in the world economy and security and the military's expanding role beyond

China's local sovereignty issues. China's interests are extending globally. Reported Chinese

---

[165]Ibid., 10-11.
[166]Ibid., 23-24.

41

military modernization and increase in spending shows that the Chinese military may soon be capable of extending operations into the Arctic region.[167]

Scenario Development

Forecasting the near-future Arctic region and the possibility of increased tension must account for numerous variables. The changing climate, potential resource wealth, and trends of increased activity and interest among Arctic and non-Arctic states leading to competition or cooperation are the variables for developing scenarios. The methods for the developed scenarios is scenario-planning approaches commonly used in military and business planning in forecasting. First is the environmental and problem framing with survey of literature on receding ice, potential hydrocarbon reserves, and strategic context of the Arctic region. The framework for scenario planning used in this study is based on the framework described by authors and strategic planning experts Paul J.H. Schoemaker in *Scenario Planning: A Tool for Strategic Thinking*,[168] and Peter Schwartz in, *The Art of the Long View*.[169] Shoemaker's initial steps of defining the scope, identifying major stakeholders, and identifying basic trends[170] as well as Schwartz's scrutinizing key forces, driving forces, and indicators,[171] correlate with the work on environmental and problem framing. The scope defined for the scenarios are the near future of ten years from the present. The information and time parameters allows for the forming of

---

[167]Peoples Republic of China, Office of the State Council, *The Diversified Employment of China's Armed Forces* (Bèijing: Office of the State Council, 2013), 4.

[168]Schoemaker, Paul J.H., "Scenario Planning: A Tool for Strategic Thinking," *Sloan Management Review* (1995): 27-30.

[169]Schwartz, Peter, *The Art of the Long View* (New York: Currency Doubleday, 1991), 226-234.

[170]Schoemaker, "Scenario Planning," 28-29.

[171]Schwartz, *The Art of the Long View*, 227-228.

42

scenarios.[172] The initial scenario themes, the next steps scenario planning, correlate to the dependent variables of receding ice levels, increase of viable economic opportunities, and state-actor approaches.[173] The increased economic opportunities include the opening sea routes and untapped resource deposits in the Arctic region. The themes are from a status quo with slower climate change and revealed economic potential to rapid changes of receding ice and opening economic opportunities.

RESEARCH METHODOLOGY

This study is a qualitative analysis of variables to develop proposed scenarios of potential outcomes related to tension or crisis in the Arctic region. Increases in commercial and military activity in the Arctic region, seeking to secure or exploit economic opportunities, correlates with the speed of climate change impacts of receding ice. This correlation represents one dependent variable in scenario planning. The anticipated approaches of state and non-state actors in response to the impacts of climate change represent the other dependent variable in scenario planning. These are categorized as either competitive or cooperative as states seek to preserve or further their self interests in the region. The outcome variable these 2 dependent variables are increased regional tension or conflict – see table 1. This study cannot account for all dependent variables within and outside the Arctic region affecting the outcome variable. This study seeks to create scenarios that forecast rather than predict the near future state of the Arctic region.

---

[172]Schoemaker, "Scenario Planning," 29-30.

[173]Schwartz, *The Art of the Long View*, 230-231.

Equation			State and Non-State Actor Approaches (DV2)	
Outcome Variable (OV)	Dependent Variable (DV1)	Dependent Variable (DV2)		
			Competitive	Cooperative
Regional Climate Change (DV1)	Fast (Near ice-free Arctic within a decade higher economic activity)		Arctic Crisis High Crisis Potential (resources, transit, sovereignty disputes, non-Arctic nation competition)	Maritime Cooperation Medium Crisis Potential (accessible sea routes, resource exploitation)
	Slow (Ice-free Arctic beyond decade lower economic activity)		Enduring Arctic Tension Medium Crisis Potential (enduring resource and sovereignty disputes)	Status Quo Low Crisis Potential (international disinterest and status quo)

Table 1: Truth table of potential outcomes related to the effects of dependent variables and the conditional variable.

ANALYSIS

The scenarios developed in this study to answer the relevant question of potential regional conflict derive from the trends of key variables affecting the Arctic region and its geopolitics in the near future. The question of potential Arctic regional conflict precipitates from significant changes of the key variables of receding ice from climate change, with increased viable economic opportunities, and state and non-state approaches to further their interests over the past decade. These identified variables generate the four scenarios forecasting trends of Arctic tension and conflict over the next decade. The four scenarios in table 1 – Status Quo, Enduring Arctic Tension, Maritime Cooperation, and Arctic Crisis – are grouped based on the anticipated relevance of each variable related to the outcome variable. The two middle scenarios, Enduring Arctic Tension, and Maritime Cooperation, are examined first. Both scenarios involve a future with some tension over sea passages and natural resources, but within the capacity for multi-national cooperation. The two more extreme scenarios, Arctic Crisis, and Arctic Status Quo, show an Arctic region of crisis leading to conflict and a tranquil Arctic with few commercial or military interests by nations. Arctic Crisis is the scenario with the least cooperation by nations or relevance of international regimes. However, international regimes are not irrelevant in mitigating conflict in the Arctic Crisis scenario. The Status Quo scenario involves such little activity to make international regime intervention unnecessary.

The time scope, previously defined, of the proposed scenarios is ten years as the variables are continuations of observed trends from the previous ten years, 2004 to present. Observing trends beyond the ten-year time scope is increasingly inaccurate due to uncertainties of changes of the future Arctic climate, anticipated demand and availability of resources, and other difficult to measure uncertainties such as internal variables within state and non-state actors. Scenarios qualitatively measuring potential conflict over the next ten years are most plausible for decision makers and planners to best anticipate future trends in the Arctic region and mitigate arising tension between Arctic and non-Arctic stakeholders.

<u>Proposed Scenarios</u>

Scenario I: Enduring Arctic Tension

This is a scenario of enduring tension among Arctic and non-Arctic nations still coveting their share of potential natural resource wealth. The economic impacts of Arctic ice recession is less dramatic in this future. Potential hydrocarbon reserves are still worthy of nations' interests, but still very difficult to reach or achieve profitability. The two waterways of the NWP and NSR are difficult to traverse with significant ice floes obstructing shipping. This mitigates the interest in the NWP and NSR as opportunities for commercial shipping and reduces the urgency of building infrastructure, safety and rescue capabilities, or increased security by littoral Arctic nations. Enduring high global demand for hydrocarbon resources may incentivize Arctic exploration and exploitation despite high operating challenges and costs. Depletion of other, easily extracted, global reserves would increasingly draw energy corporations and countries

45

willing to incur the higher cost of exploiting Arctic resources. Competition among Arctic littoral and non-Arctic nations continues.

The near future Arctic region according to this scenario is a competitive environment as nations are incentivized to gain or maintain their share of the Arctic region's opportunities. The competition for resources is still managed by a multi-lateral framework of power. Other still interested Arctic nations counter-balance any other powerful nation attempting to gain hegemonic status and assert Arctic dominance. Militaries are still incentivized to improve their Arctic capabilities and enhance their operational reach into their northern borders and shores for security.

Russia may act unilaterally to begin exploration and extraction operations in the disputed international waters of the Arctic. It would increase its Arctic military presence as proposed in its 2008 strategy, continuing intimidating bomber flights against neighboring nations. Acting unilaterally, Russia may not see incentives in formally seeking approval for its territorial claims and diplomatic resolution of its share of the Arctic region. A nationalist Russia may seek to assert its dominance as a great Arctic power ignoring other nations' claims and the UNCLOS.

China may assert itself more into the Arctic region as its economic and military power grows, with its growing demand for hydrocarbon resources. China would seek to increase its clout on the Arctic Council. It would apply for permanent member status from observer on the council. The greater role in the Arctic Council allows China better access to the Arctic region for hydrocarbon and other resource exploration and extraction operations.

International forums for managing the region such as the Arctic Council and UN, through UNCLOS, remain relevant to nations seeking international legitimacy for their territorial claims. Overall, the group of littoral Arctic nations, and other non-Arctic nations, with international regimes, could manage any potential aggressiveness by any power. The multi-lateral framework of power through international regimes can manage a nationalist Russia, or resource-hungry

China attempting to secure more than its share of the region's wealth. Any persistent disputes over resources or territory, anticipated by this scenario, are within the capacity of international regimes to manage before reaching to a level of crisis.

The indicators leading to this outcome are more competitive behavior among the three powerful Arctic nations – Russia, Canada, and United States. Russian bomber flights near neighboring nations' airspace may increase. Diplomatic rows may develop, debated in the UN or Arctic Council, over hydrocarbon exploration and extraction in disputed territory. A notable indicator of this scenario is accelerated commercial and military activity and coercion by the rising non-Arctic nation, China.

Scenario II: Maritime Cooperation

Economic impacts from climate change in this scenario are more dramatic, anticipating increased activity. Receding ice further opens the NWP and NSR for commercial and military maritime traffic, increasing their economic viability. Operating challenges for increased commercial shipping remain, necessitating improved infrastructure and safety mechanisms.[174] The other variable of national approaches is cooperative in this scenario. International regimes of the Arctic Council and the UN are relevant for mitigating disputes as countries encroach into the Arctic region. The incentives for cooperation between nations from the international management of new commercial waterways create an eventual cooperative near future in this scenario.

Tensions over access of the passages would increase as Canada and Russia continue to assert their sovereignty over the waterways. Other Arctic and non-Arctic nations, such as the United States and China, would assert that the passages are international routes open to all nations. Opening the Arctic routes can also lead to greater cooperation and regulation by

---

[174]L. Brigham, et al., ed., *Arctic Marine Shipping Assessment 2009 Report*, 32-34.

international law in the ungoverned region. Nations' governments and militaries would cooperate across boundaries to improve the maritime infrastructure and emergency response capability of the busier sea routes recommended by the AMSA report. The economic incentive of opening the waterways could ease the nationalist stance of Canada and Russia. Militaries would also enhance their operational reach capabilities in the Arctic region, improving bases and their Arctic training capabilities. The role of increased militarization would be more cooperative to collectively ensure security of commercial traffic and prevent terrorism than a cold war-like stand off.

This scenario highlights the relevance of multi-lateral efforts of the Arctic Council and the UN. Such inter-governmental forums can mitigate tension among Arctic and non-Arctic nations and allow the shared economic benefits of the opened passages. Maritime issues tend to lead toward international cooperation even among rivals. The United States, in this scenario, would increase involvement as a power broker in compromises between Canadian and Russian sovereignty and international use of the Arctic passages. Tension between maritime nations seeking use of the NWP and NSR would be short-lived with the greater incentive of cooperation. Canada and Russia as caretakers of the routes, and the United States and China as advocates of international routes, would realize the risks of acting unilaterally in securing the passages for their self interests. The opportunity costs of denying the routes to international commerce would be too great to risk maintaining tension. The leading indicators of this scenario are increased cooperation among Arctic littoral nations in regulating the opened waterways. The owners of the NWP and NSR, Canada and Russia, cooperate in implementing the safety and infrastructure recommendations by the AMSA in opening the sea passages.

Scenario III: Arctic Crisis

The Arctic Crisis scenario is an anticipated future of dramatic economic and military impacts in the Arctic region. Both the opening waterways for increased maritime use and rush to

48

exploit Arctic hydrocarbon resources are increasingly relevant in this scenario. The NWP and NSR waterways are viable commercial and military routes within a decade. Littoral Arctic nations and global commercial interests will need to plan for development of the routes and agree on sovereign control or global openness. Global demand for hydrocarbon resources will remain high and increase from depletion of other deposits. The consequential higher prices for oil and natural gas increases potential profitability and challenges energy security for nations. The incentives are greater for nations seeking greater claims to deposits in the ungoverned or disputed areas of the Arctic. Exploration of the region confirms assessments by the USGS of vast amounts of oil and natural gas in the disputed continental shelves and undersea ridges beneath the Arctic Ocean. The expansive economic opportunities of sea routes and resource wealth creates an incentive for stronger Arctic and non-Arctic nations to apply their power toward unilaterally securing their share of the Arctic region. This is the more competitive scenario as state actors potentially clash in the proverbial "Great Game," over the Arctic region. Multi-national forums and international law are less capable of managing the increased tension and potentially cast to irrelevance. The Arctic region in this scenario is a highly contentious arena for nations seeking advantage in control of the sea passages and hydrocarbon resources. Tension over the ice-free sea passages may escalate as nations begin to increase their regional naval presence to protect or aggressively assert their access to the waterways. The potential for tensions over security and sovereignty are high as nations seek competitive approaches to securing their Arctic interests.

The viability of the sea routes forces important decisions for the governments of Russia and Canada - both littoral Arctic nations holding the dominant share of the NSR and NWP. Russia will face pressures over its share of the NSR along its northern coastline. The economic incentive of opening the NSR versus Russian security may lead to a limited opening of the route to allies of Russia. An example is a bi-lateral Sino-Russian agreement allowing commerce from Chinese ports through the NSR to European and Eastern North American markets.

A disaffected Russia in this scenario can be incentivized towards better cooperation through "side payments," – a concept within game theory applied to state actor behavior.[175] Side payments are transfers of wealth that "enlarge the scope of cooperation," while allowing the participants to effectively threaten or blackmail each other.[176] The other Arctic participants can work backstage agreements with Russia, achieving compromise on use of the NSR or shared access to Arctic resource wealth. This could occur amid frontstage threatening and rhetoric. Side payments as incentivization are also regarded as "appeasement." It is similar to the policy of allowing pre-World War II Nazi Germany to annex part of Czechoslovakia to avoid conflict.[177] An environment of crisis with an aggressive Russia may necessitate side payments to postpone rather than prevent conflict. Arctic neighbors can buy time to strengthen their military posture for better advantage.

Canada would continue its position that the NWP is a sovereign, and not an international waterway. This position risks contention with Canada's ally, the United States. Canada and the United States will debate over the ownership of the NWP. The two nations will need to create a bi-lateral agreement managing both Canada's sovereignty concerns with the US position that the sea passage is an international waterway open to all commerce. Failing to meet an agreement favoring international access, the United States would act unilaterally using the NWP in violation of Canadian sovereignty claims. A rejection of Canada's 2013 territorial claim may force the country extend its military reach and occupation of resource deposits or risk Russian encroachment.

The rising contention over the Arctic could lead to another build-up of US presence as its

---

[175]Martin Shubik, *On Gaming and Game Theory* (Santa Monica: Rand Corporation, 1971), 14.

[176]Ibid.

[177]Geoffrey Parker, ed., *Cambridge Illustrated History of Warfare* (New York: Cambridge University Press, 1995), 304.

own interests are challenged. The US Government may renewed efforts to sign the UNCLOS, or decide to act unilaterally in securing its interests. The United States advocates for international access of the Arctic region, and promotes the UNCLOS despite being a non-signatory to the agreement. Unbounded by the UNCLOS, the United States could decide to apply the Truman Administration's claim to any continental shelf resources discovered.

Non-Arctic nations with maritime commercial interests would further act to try to open the NWP through forums like the Arctic Council. The incentive of an ice-free NWP would spur nations like China and European nations to increase their power in the council from observer to permanent member status. The ice-free sea routes and their economic incentives may generate multi-lateral cooperation through international forums for access to all nations. The waterways can also generate more tension in the Arctic region as other nations join the US position, advocating for greater international accessibility.

There is some cooperation among littoral Arctic and non-Arctic nations, in this scenario. Owners of the waterways may compromise over sovereign control with limited opening of the routes or bi-lateral agreements. Littoral Arctic nations may form blocs, like Russia and China, or Canada and the United States, rather than working through international forums of the UN or Arctic Council on opening the sea routes to maritime commerce. NATO involvement would increase as 3 of its members, the United States, Canada, and Norway are threatened by Russian or Chinese aggressiveness. Cooperative efforts between NATO and Russia, recently suspended with the 2014 crisis with Ukraine, are less likely to help reduce tensions. An operational increase of NATO forces in the Arctic, naval patrols, basing, or increased exercises would generate fears from Russia of containment. Russia continues to fear NATO encroachment along its western borders and former Soviet satellites. An increase in NATO activity in Russia's north is an engine for crisis. International forums and agreements to include the Arctic Council, UNCLOS, and AMSA must adapt in this scenario. To avoid irrelevance, the international regimes would adapt into security forums, working toward preventing and resolving conflict in the Arctic region. This would mean more importance to international forums than economic cooperation, climate change, and conservation.

The Arctic region becomes more militarized in this scenario. Arctic and non-Arctic militaries will increase their capabilities and develop operational approaches to secure their interests. Russia, Canada, and the United States have written national strategies regarding their interests in the Arctic, including proposals to increase regional military capabilities. Arctic and sub Arctic ports such as Murmansk, Vladivostok, Anchorage, Reykjavik, or Oslo would see an increase in naval activity with the commercial boom of the maritime passages. China may try to assert its own presence in the region as it's military capabilities grow. China's current overtures to Iceland[178] and Greenland[179] could later be attempts to attain places and bases for a forward Arctic presence. Military forces positioned near the SLOC openings of the Bering Strait or Atlantic accesses would be vital to securing nations' interests or enforcing international norms. The remoteness and extremes of Arctic geography are particular challenges to developing operational approaches. The littoral Arctic nations, despite sharing sovereign territory in the region, must plan to establish and maintain an enduring operational reach and basing in the Arctic. Militaries face enormous logistics challenges as they try to increase and maintain their operational reach into the remote Arctic region.

The leading indicators of this scenario are more competitive and unilateral activity by nations in securing their self interests. The owners of the sea passages become more exclusive and nationalist in their approach toward maritime use of the waterways. Nations may form blocs, such as Russia and China, in allowing use of sea routes, excluding other nations. The United

---

[178]The Economist, "Warming up to Iceland," *The Economist*, Analects, April 17, 2013.
[179]Stephen Blank, "China's Arctic Strategy," *The Diplomat*, June 20, 2013, 1.

States and Canada may form a counterbalance with increased military and diplomatic cooperation. International regimes to include the UN and Arctic Council are less relevant in mitigating the growing challenges of managing the use of the Arctic region. NATO involvement may increase in the Arctic region, securing the interests of its 3 Arctic nations and the northern security of Europe against a nationalist Russia.

Scenario IV: Arctic Status Quo

This scenario is an anticipated future where changes to the Arctic geography and economic potential are slower than estimated. Recession of the Arctic ice is slower, according to climate change models projecting extensive recession beyond 10 years.[180] Enough ice would remain in the sea passages even during the summer months making maritime travel very treacherous except for specialized icebreaker ships. The danger to commercial shipping, and slower movement through the NWP and NSR would be unprofitable. The costs of building infrastructure and security and safety capabilities along the routes prove cost prohibitive for caretakers of the routes. The amount of accessible hydrocarbon resources in the Arctic for this scenario would also be much less than estimated. The slower receding ice makes accessibility of potential deposits cost prohibitive. Market forces of world demand for hydrocarbons are also less with increased development of alternative energy resources. The lower global demand for hydrocarbon resources makes the difficulty of Arctic resource extraction further unprofitable in this scenario. Geopolitically, the Arctic region would not see an increase in interest or activity from Arctic or non-Arctic nations. The smaller incentive for encroachment into the Arctic leads to less need for international regimes to mitigate tension. Any lingering territorial disputes receive little attention, and remain as curiosities of international politics. Disputes within the Arctic

---

[180]Lisa Alexander et. al., *"Climate Change 2013: The Physical Science Basis,"* SPM-17.

region would remain fully in the regulatory capacities of bi-lateral agreement or international law. This scenario anticipates very little tension or competition over economic opportunities.

The state of Arctic security in the near future of this scenario is a status quo as the name suggests. The brief increase in exploration for resources and military activity in the Arctic region would subside as geographic and economic realities become apparent. The search for viable resources produces diminished returns for Arctic-interested nations and corporations, and a reduction in commercial and military activity would ensue. The multilateral groups of the Arctic Council and the UN would serve to manage issues related to conservation, long term affects of climate change, and indigenous peoples. Near future economic distribution and security concerns among the littoral Arctic nations would be fewer and less significant. Outer non-Arctic nations would seek economic opportunities elsewhere, only looking toward the Arctic for scientific research. Future, unanticipated political climates of Russia, Canada, or the United States would lead to a continued ebb and flow of interest in their northern borders. A still nationalist Russia could decide to continue antagonizing bomber over-flights near neighboring nations' airspace. Border and territorial issues to United States/Russia and Canada/Hans Island could remain unsettled. There would be such little interest that these disputes would persist, if not, forgotten.

Arctic nations' operational approaches could include maintaining military forces in their sub-Arctic territories and bases such as Murmansk, Fairbanks, or the Yukon Territory. Patrols and monitoring of their northern borders would be less than proposed in their respective Arctic national strategies. Coast guard forces would not develop significant rescue and recovery operations, or combined multinational safety capabilities with the absence of human activity. Arctic nations would continue to struggle to maintain minimal fleets of icebreaker ships to ensure some access through the polar ice. The leading indicators leading to this scenario are reduced commercial and military activity in the Arctic region. The harsh climatic conditions and remoteness keep human activity limited to indigenous people and scientific research.

Summary

The changes in the Arctic geography due to climate change are leading to increased interest by Arctic and non-Arctic nations. The near future could be a boom in commercial activity whether its opening sea-lanes, hydrocarbon deposits, or both sets of economic opportunities. The anticipated commercial boom generates increased security concerns by Arctic littoral nations wanting to stake claims and protect their territory. A growing economic, non-Arctic nation, like China, vies for greater influence and access to potential economic opportunities. All interested nations must weigh the costs and benefits of increasing their activity and reach into the costly remote lands and waters of the north. The requirements of opening commercially viable waterways may increase international cooperation to build infrastructure, safety, and multilateral security. The potential wealth of the region and increased security concerns may lead nations to take a competitive stance protecting their self interests. The Arctic Council faces challenges of adapting from a forum addressing conservation to more like a security cooperation organization. Arctic littoral nations and non-Arctic nations currently favor wielding their power through international bodies and treaties like UNCLOS. In these scenarios, the trend of cooperation could shift to competition by the more powerful nations and expansion into the Arctic for regional hegemony. Incentives to seize Arctic riches and opportunities for themselves could overturn trends of diplomacy and power sharing. All actors in these scenarios, governmental and inter-governmental, must determine their future position in the new Arctic region.

CONCLUSION

The littoral nations of the Arctic region face potential challenges and opportunities due to transformations from climate change. The receding polar ice open new sea passages and allow easier access to undersea hydrocarbon resources. The five Arctic nations and outer non-Arctic nations are developing strategies and increasing their commercial and military activity in the region. The potential outcomes of greater economic and military interest and nations' activity are from a stable status quo of less activity to a "Great Game" scenario of high activity and potential for competition or conflict. For each near-future forecast of Arctic regional geopolitics, miscalculations can exacerbate tension toward conflict, or able statecraft can further cooperation and avert crisis. The outcomes leading to greater tension into crisis, or conflict – particularly the "Arctic Crisis" scenario – are inimical to US interests of stability and international access to the Arctic region.

The future capability of US military, diplomatic, and economic power may be very different, affecting stability of the Arctic region. A reduced role in the Arctic by the United States, either through disinterest or capability, could create a vacuum allowing other powers to assert dominance. The future power of the Arctic and non-Arctic nations of Russia, Canada, and China are equally uncertain. The "side payment" method of incentivizing a disaffected Russia can temporarily ease tensions leading to conflict. A greater distribution of the potential economic benefit of the Arctic by the other actors, could prove effective to "enlarge the scope of cooperation."[181] Such means – diplomatic, informational, military and economic – may prove highly effective in averting a future state of conflict, and securing vital US security interests in the Arctic region.

---

[181]Martin Shubik, *On Gaming and Game Theory* (Santa Monica: Rand Corporation, 1971), 14.

Recommendations

An increased role and presence by the United States and its Arctic allies is important to a peaceful Arctic. This begins with furthering the effort in the US government to sign the UNCLOS. Strengthening the relevance and power of the international community to manage the Arctic helps build the Arctic as more equitable for nations, and reducing the need for conflict. International groups like the UNCLOS and the Arctic Council have great influence in the regulation of the race for the Arctic region and its riches. The continuity of the international management of the Arctic over any one or group of powerful nations is a stabilizing factor to keeping Arctic peace. The idea of international equity of the Arctic region must mitigate competition, unilateralism and exclusiveness of some Arctic powers. The United States and Canada should negotiate a bi-lateral agreement over the open use of the NWP for international commerce. The demands of geography and standard maritime practice help move neighboring Arctic nations to cooperate and build systems of security and safety for commercial shipping in the sea passages. Arctic security issues should be managed between the Arctic littoral nations and the Arctic Council. Increased NATO involvement may only exacerbate a potential crisis reducing Russian incentives for cooperation. Russian security fears on its western borders in Europe would repeat as it senses NATO encroachment in their north.

For developing operational approaches, the US military can enhance its presence and reach into the Arctic region to ensure American commitment to a stable Arctic region. The current and near future budget realities of US defense are challenges to a renewed American commitment to Arctic defense. The United States would potentially pay a higher price long-term by a retraction of US military forces in Alaska and the Arctic region. Establishing a new combatant command dedicated to the Arctic region as recommended by some experts may not be the answer. Certainly, unity of command appears challenging with Arctic responsibility divided among the Pacific, European, and Northern commands.[182] The US Army's regionally aligned forces concept should encompass the Arctic region. Brigades aligned to the Arctic region can train with Alaskan-based units in existing training facilities to enhance Arctic operational capabilities. US military forces, using existing Arctic basing, can improve their operational reach against the vastness and extreme geography of the region. The militaries of the United States and its Arctic allies of Canada, Norway, and non-Arctic allies can increase their inter-operability through training exercises like Operation NANOOK in Canada. The existing partnerships among neighboring Arctic nations is sufficient to manage future tension while ensuring security. This reduces the need for greater NATO involvement in the region, which may exacerbate Russian security fears. Strong military capabilities and alliances, regulated by international law and forums, ensure future Arctic regional stability. A lawful, cooperative, multi-lateral Arctic framework dis-incentivizes potential expansionist or hegemonic ideas by any one great Arctic or non-Arctic power.

---

[182]Michael J. Peeler, "Command and Control: Toward Arctic Unity of Command and Unity of Effort" (monograph, School of Advanced Military Studies, 2011), 33-34.

BIBLIOGRAPHY

Alberta Energy. "Facts and Statistics." www.energy.alberta.ca (accessed March 19, 2014).

Alexander, Lisa, Simon Allen, Nathaniel L. Bindoff, Francois-Marie Breon, John Church, Ulrich Cubasch, Seita Emori, Piers Forster, Pierre Friedlingstein, Nathan Gillett, Jonathan Gregory, Dennis Hartmann, Eystein Jansen, Ben Kirtman, Reto Knutti, Krishna Kumar Kanikicharia, Peter Lemke, Jochem Marotzke, Valerie Masson-Delmotte, Gerald Meehl, Igor Mokhov, Silong Piao, Gian-Kasper Plattner, Qin Dahe, Venkatachalam Ramaswamy, David Randall, Monika Rhein, Maisa Rojas, Christopher Sabine, Drew Shindell, Thomas F. Stocker, Lynne Talley, David Vaughan, Shang-Ping Xie. *Working Group I Contribution to the IPCC Fifth Assessment Report Climate Change 2013: The Physical Science Basis, Summary for Policymakers*. Geneva: Intergovernmental Panel on Climate Change, 2013.

Antrim, Caitlyn L. "The Arctic in Twentieth-Century Geopolitics." In *Arctic Security in the Age of Climate Change* edited by James Kraska, 107-128. New York: Cambridge, 2011.

Arctic Council. *Declaration on the Establishment of the Arctic Council*. Ottawa: Arctic Council, 1996.

---. "Environment and People." www.arctic-council.org (accessed March 9, 2014).

---. "Member States." www.arctic-council.org. (accessed November 8, 2013).

---. "Observers." www.arctic-council.org (Accessed March 27, 2014).

---. "Peoples of the Arctic." www.arctic-council.org (accessed March 9, 2014).

Balasevicius, Tony. "Towards a Canadian Forces Arctic Operating Concept." *Canadian Military Journal*, (Spring 2011): 21-31.

Berkman, Paul Arthur. "Preventing an Arctic Cold War." *New York Times*. March 12, 2013.

Bobbitt, Daniel R. "Canada's 2009 Northern Strategy: Cold War Policy in a Warming Arctic." Monograph, School of Advanced Military Studies, 2010.

Borgerson, Scott G. "Arctic Meltdown, The Economic and Security Implications of Global Warming." *Foreign Affairs*. www.foreignaffairs.com (accessed April 16, 2014).

---. "The Coming Arctic Boom, As the Ice Melts, the Region Heats up." *Foreign Affairs*, (July/August 2013): 76-90.

---. "The Great Game Moves North, As the Arctic Melts, Countries Vie for Control." *Foreign Affairs*. www.foreignaffairs.com (accessed April 16, 2014).

Stephen Blank. "China's Arctic Strategy." *The Diplomat*, June 20, 2013.

Blank, Stephen J. *Russia in the Arctic*. Carlisle: Strategic Studies Institute, US Army War College, 2011.

Brigham, Lawson W. "The Challenges and Security Issues of Arctic Marine Transport." In *Arctic Security in the Age of Climate Change* Edited by James Kraska, 20-32. New York: Cambridge, 2011.

Brigham L., R. McCalla, E. Cunningham, W. Barr, D. VenderZwaag, A. Chircop, V. M. Santos-Pedro, R. MacDonald, S. Harder, B. Ellis, J. Snyder, H. Huntington, H. Skjoldal, M. Gold, M. Williams, T. Wojhan, J. Falkingham. *Arctic Marine Shipping Assessment 2009 Report.* Reykjavik: Arctic Council, 2009.

Bush, George W. *National Security Presidential Directive and Homeland Security Presidential Directive 66*. Washington, DC: The White House, 2009.

Byers, Michael. *Who Owns the Arctic?: Understanding Sovereignty Disputes in the North*. Vancouver: Douglas and McIntyre, 2010.

Central Intelligence Agency. "The World Factbook: Arctic Ocean." www.cia.gov (accessed November 8, 2013).

Peoples Republic of China, Office of the State Council. *The Diversified Employment of China's Armed Forces*. Beijing: Office of the State Council, 2013.

Chinese Arctic and Antarctic Administration. "Chinese Arctic Yellow River Station." www.chinare.gov.cn (accessed March 27, 2014).

Cohen, Ariel. "Russia in the Arctic: Challenges to US Energy and Geopolitics in the High North." In *Russia in the Arctic*, edited by Stephen J. Blank. Carlisle: US Army War College, 2011.

Conley, Heather and Jamie Kraut. *US Strategic Interests in the Arctic*. Washington, DC: CSIS, 2010.

Cole, Dermot. *North to the Future: The Alaska Story, 1959-2009*. Kenmore: Epicenter, 2008.

Collins, Gabe. "China Looms Over Russian Far East." *The Diplomat*, June 22, 2011.

The Economist. "Warming up to Iceland." *The Economist*, Analects, April 17, 2013.

Goldenberg, Suzanne. "Arctic on Track for Ice-Free Summer 'Within Decades,' Scientists Say." *The Guardian*, September 20, 2013.

Golts, Alexandr. "The Arctic: A Clash of Interests or Clash of Ambitions," In *Russia in the Arctic*, edited by Stephen J. Blank, 43-62. Carlisle: US Army War College, 2011.

Hatton, Sonny T. "Canadian Unilateralism in the Arctic: Using Scenario Planning to Help Canada Achieve its Strategic Goals in the North." Monograph, School of Advanced Military Studies, 2013.

International Monetary Fund. "World Economic Outlook Database, April 2013, China." www.imf.org (accessed 27 March 27, 2014).

Joint Base Elmendorf-Richardson. "Fact Sheet: Military History in Alaska, 1867-2000." www.jber.af.mil (accessed August 3, 2013).

Kraska, James. *Arctic Security in an Age of Climate Change*. Cambridge: Cambridge University Press, 2011.

Krasner, Stephen D. "Structural Causes and Regime Consequences: Regimes as Intervening Variables." In *International Regimes*, ed., Stephen D. Krasner. Ithaca: Cornell University, 1983.

Laruelle, Marlene. "Russian Military Presence in the High North: Projection of Power and Capacities of Action." In, *Russia in the Arctic*, edited by Stephen J. Blank, 63-89. Carlisle: US Army War College, 2011.

Maruyev, A. Yu. Col. "Russia and the USA in Confrontation: Military and Political Aspects." *Military Thought, Monthly Theoretical Journal of the Russian General Staff* (2013).

Medvedev, Dmitry. *National Security Strategy Russia 2020, Decree No. 537*. Moscow: Security Council of the Russian Federation, May 12, 2009.

Ministry of Foreign Affairs, Canada. "Canada's Foreign Policy." www.international.gc.ca (accessed on April 16, 2014).

Ministry of Public Works and Government Services, Canada. *Canada's Northern Strategy, Our North, Our Heritage, Our Future*. Ottawa: Government of Canada, 2009.

NANA Regional Corporation, Inc. "Red Dog Operations." www.reddogalaska.com (accessed March 17, 2014).

National Snow and Ice Data Center. "A better year for the cryoshpere." www.nsidc.org (Accessed March 9, 2014).

---. "All About Arctic Climatology and Meteorology." www.nsidc.org (accessed November 8, 2013).

---. "Arctic Sea Ice News & Analysis." www.nsidc.org (accessed March 9, 2014).

---. "Ice thickness and age," in, *A better year for the cryoshpere*, NSIDC. www.nsidc.org (accessed 9 March 2014).

---. "Our Sponsors." www.nsidc.org (accessed March 9, 2014).

Nielson, Jonathan M. *Armed Forces on a Northern Frontier: The Military in Alaska's History, 1867-1987*. Westport: Praeger, 1988.

North American Aerospace Defense Command. "NORAD Agreement." www.norad.mil
(accessed 19 March 19, 2014).

---. "About NORAD: NORAD Agreement." www.norad.mil (accessed November 8, 2013).

Obama, Barack. "National Strategy for the Arctic Region." The White House.
www.whitehouse.gov (accessed August 3, 2013).

O'Rourke, Ronald. *Changes in the Arctic: Background and Issues for Congress*. Washington,
DC: Government Accountability Office, 2011.

Parker Geoffrey. *Cambridge Illustrated History, Warfare*. New York: Cambridge University
Press, 1995.

Peeler, Michael J. "Command and Control: Toward Arctic Unity of Command and Unity of
Effort." Monograph, School of Advanced Military Studies, 2011.

Pendleton, John H. *Arctic Capabilities*. Washington, DC: Government Accountability Office,
2012.

Rainwater, Shiloh. "Race to the North: China's Arctic Strategy and Its Implications." *Naval War
College Review*, vol. 66, no.2 (Spring 2013) (2013): 62-82.

Rickard, Michael B. "US Arctic Security." Research paper, Fletcher School, Tufts University,
2012.

Schoemaker, Paul J. H. "Scenario Planning: A Tool for Strategic Thinking." *Sloan Management
Review* (1995): 27-30.

Schwartz, Peter. *The Art of the Long View*. New York: Currency Doubleday, 1991.

Shubik, Martin. *On Gaming and Game Theory*. Santa Monica: Rand Corporation, 1971.

Sibley, Robert. "Arrival of China in Arctic puts Canada on Alert." *Ottowa Citizen*, October 28,
2011.

Stauffer, Peter H. *Circum-Arctic Resource Appraisal: Estimates of Undiscovered Oil and Gas
North of the Arctic Circle*. Menlo Park: USGS, 2008.

Smith, Laurence C., and Scott R. Stephenson. "New Trans-Arctic shipping routes navigable by
midcentury." *Proceedings of the National Academy of Science of the United States of
America* (2013): E1191-E1195.

United Nations. "United Nations Convention on the Law of the Sea (UNCLOS)." www.un.org
(accessed March 18, 2014).

---. "UNCLOS, Part V, Exclusive Economic Zone." www.un.org (accessed March 18, 2014).

US Army Alaska. "USARAK Organizations." www.usarak.army.mil (accessed March 26, 2014).

United States Energy Information Administration (EIA). "Arctic oil and natural gas resources." www.eia.gov (accessed August 3, 2013).

---. "World Oil Transit Chokepoints, Analysis." www.eia.gov (accessed March 9, 2014).

Waddell, Karen. *Cold War Historical Context 1951-1991*. Fort Collins: Colorado State University, 2003.

Waltz, Kenneth N. *Theory of International Politics*. Long Grove: Waveland, 1979.

Wezeman, Siemon T. *Military Capabilities in the Arctic*. Solna: Stockholm International Peace Research Institute, 2012.

Wright, David Curtis. *The Dragon Eyes the Top of the World*. Newport: US Naval War College, 2011.

---. *Panda Bear Readies to Meet Polar Bear*. Calgary: Canadian Defense and Foreign Affairs Institute, 2011.

Young, Oran R. Forward to *Arctic Security in the Age of Climate Change*. edited by James Kraska, xxi-xxvii. New York: Cambridge, 2011.

447th Fighter Group. "Arctic Reserve Units." www.477fg.afrc.af.mil (accessed March 26, 2014).